The &-Files

The

&-Files

Paul Foss

ART & TEXT 1981–2002

Rob McKenzie with Ross Chambers, Rex Butler, and Simon Rees

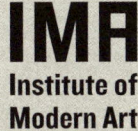

IMA
Institute of
Modern Art

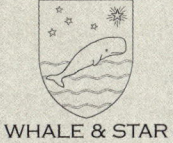

WHALE & STAR

For Sydney gallery owners Roslyn and Tony Oxley,
without whose encouragement and nurturing
ART & TEXT might never have existed.

Contents

Acknowledgments

The story behind these files is not unlike the story of their prime suspect. On December 21, 2005, I received an email from a young Melbourne artist wishing to interview me about *Art & Text*, a contemporary art magazine I published between 1984 and 2002, when I decided to close it down. Rob McKenzie, a virtual stranger, had a set of questions he wanted me to answer online. At first I was unhelpful, being somewhat shocked to learn that this level of curiosity in the magazine still existed. I proceeded to explain to him my reluctance to mull over the "facts," believing them to be mostly accidental or the outcome of larger cultural forces, which only a team of historians could unravel. I also explained that a tell-all report, although tempting, was not worth the bad publicity it would attract. But Rob would hear none of it, leaving me at a loss to find a solution.

We shouldn't forget that the history (or fable) of *Art & Text* is essentially a lesser moral tale about the Australian cultural condition as a whole, so it is already a narrative of imminent collapse or tailspin. Beginning as a small Melbourne art zine in 1981, the brainchild of a young lad about town called Paul Taylor, the magazine went on to change its identity and address many times over a twenty-year period, finally establishing itself in Los Angeles in 1999. This checkered career caused a lot of comment back home. Paul Taylor soon moved to New York, where he worked as an art critic during the 1980s and early '90s. *Art & Text*, always a problem child, stuck it out in Melbourne and then Sydney, gradually building up a modest reputation along the way. But juggling the international with the homegrown is never easy in Australian cultural politics, since success in one field is often interpreted as a slap across the face in the other. Like it or not, the magazine proved controversial.

To be sure, these were not matters I now felt ideally situated to discuss. Nor was I especially concerned to look back, because I had since started a new magazine called *artUS*, which involved a very different set of questions and regional politics. Once the interview began, however, I soon realized that I needed time to work out some ground rules for myself—telling tales out of school became my worst fear. The interview ground to a halt and was eventually ditched, and a year or so went by. Meanwhile, a successful application was made to the Australia Council for a development grant, and the project started to shape itself into a book. In due course I sat down to write Rob an "open letter" explaining the great introspection his request had caused me, how I'd needed to condition myself to remembering half-forgotten events, to figuring out what I could or could not get away with saying, and, most importantly, how I'd needed to put all rumor to rest by posting a secret file of my own.

After that delay, the interview recommenced, although it ended up being redrafted several times. Independently, I also invited two colleagues, CAC Vilnius curator Simon Rees and University of Queensland art historian Rex Butler, to send me a questionnaire, hoping to make good any omissions in the central file and to increase the cast of players. Somehow, sticking to this idea of calling others to the witness box continued to guide me. Rob contributed an essay on Paul Taylor and the early years of the magazine, as well as a catalogue raisonné. I then asked Ross Chambers, former head of the French Department at Sydney University and now retired in Ann Arbor, Michigan, to read the manuscript and write a foreword, to which he kindly consented. Just like *The X-Files*, these files truly evolved through putting the questions themselves to the test.

Throughout the entire process, Rob McKenzie played a key role in coaxing these files out of me. Thanks are also owed to Enrique Martínez Celaya at Whale & Star (Delray Beach, Florida) and Robert Leonard at the Institute of Modern Art (Brisbane, Australia) for their gracious interest in publishing them. The Australia Council generously funded the magazine and supported this project. Lastly, special thanks must go to Micah Heimlich, without whose assistance *The &-Files* might well have ended in the trash bin.

Paul Foss
Los Angeles
August 9, 2008

Foreword

It was shortsighted of me, to put it mildly. Almost as soon as I gave up and left Australia to live in the United States, everything began to happen. I would come back to Sydney on slightly wistful visits and have lunch with a few people before heading for Gleebooks, armed with my reading list, to catch up a bit and further my education. I soon began referring to those years as "the ampersand years," in recognition of the flagship role played by the extraordinary magazine whose editorial history *The &-Files* vividly retraces. Each of its numbers, as Paul Foss says, was a bolt from the blue. And it waved that cheeky typographical sign like some kind of quirky banner signaling that something very lively was underway among Australia's artists, thinkers, and activists.

So it wasn't long before I also began to read the provocative squiggle as an appropriately messy metaphor for the very tangled intellectual community that was emerging, with all its connections and conjunctions of different projects and agendas, and all its theoretical, aesthetic, political, and cultural trajectories. Paul Foss himself—with his encyclopedic education and extraordinary range of interests, his translator's and editor's skills, and his ability to learn from his friends and acquaintances (as from a philosopher of science like Bachelard, a lively theorist like the early Baudrillard, or the extraordinary intellectual figure of Walter Benjamin)—looks to me now, in retrospect, like a personification of that community, and indeed (if I may risk a metaphor he may not much appreciate), one of its most active personal ampersands.

Consider what was going on then. Republicanism had the wind in its sails, as did the Indigenous land-rights movement; the sexual revolution was upon us (or at least around the corner); multiculturalism seemed a reality. A film industry was up and going, and making interesting movies. I remember walking one day into the University of New South Wales library and falling under the spell of dot painting from the central desert and bark painting from the north. Theater was lively, opera was approaching the status of a spectator sport, local bands and performers were making a mark in popular culture, and "authentic performance" was still thrilling to classical audiences. Meanwhile, an Australian cultural studies was being invented in and out of the universities, and the intelligentsia was putting into play a host of theoretical ideas and new intellectual toolkits as fast as they emerged, whether in Australia or elsewhere. To the dismay of the public press, the French post-structuralism it reviled was leading the pack, and a host of heady new words—semiotics, simulacrum, deconstruction, discourse—were in active circulation.

Feminism too was breaking out everywhere. And gay emancipation had blossomed just in time, alas, for the community to have to mobilize its forces—

backed by the government in some cases—against the sudden scourge of HIV/
AIDS. Certain cities were internationalizing fast, and doing so culturally and
intellectually as well as commercially. Sydney, in particular, was discovering a talent
for throwing parties for the world, even as Juan Davila's exhibitions were still being
visited by the police and fulminated against in the usual places, and Eric Michaels
was developing a theory of—above all—Aboriginal and gay "unbecoming" as a
necessary strategy of opposition. So Mardi Gras flourished in a very Sydney style by
miraculously combining unbecomingness and having a good time, oppositionality
and international fame. It all seemed to culminate somehow—the life-giving new
ideas, the political and cultural oppositionality, the partying—in the nose-thumbing
Aboriginal counter-celebrations of the 1988 Bicentennial (which, to my mind, make
the tamer festivities of the 2000 Olympic Games look, in retrospect, like the era's
swansong). For those "ampersand years" are no more, it seems, and *Art & Text*,
their constant goad and stimulant, published its last number in 2002. With judicious
prodding from Rob McKenzie, Paul Foss carries out here what he calls an "autopsy"
of his memories.

I, in turn, am left reflecting on the relatively rare privilege I've enjoyed, the
privilege not just of learning from but of being educated by people significantly
younger than myself. To be educated means to be changed, to undergo a significant
reorientation of the direction you had been pursuing. Thanks to people like the
three Pauls—Paul Patton, Paul Taylor, and Paul Foss (whom at the time I did
not know and tended to confuse a bit like the members of another well-known
trinity)—and thanks also to many others mentioned in these pages who were my
former students sometimes, colleagues too on occasion, and always valued friends, I
got an unanticipated *Bildung*: a thorough midlife reshaping of who I was, what I was
thinking, and where I thought myself to be going.

That realization came to me as I read this book, along with many new insights
into a fascinating and important period of Australian cultural history; one or two
bits of good gossip; and a deepened understanding of what it means to practice
the twin trades of translating and editing, trades that have a lot in common with
my own lifetime employment as a teacher. Reader, since you have picked up this
valuable little book, I wish you equal profit. It's as good as guaranteed.

Ross Chambers
May 2008

Introduction:
Explicit Content, The Early Issues

Rob McKenzie

The art department at Melbourne High School in South Yarra where I went to school had a small number of early issues of *Art & Text*. I remember thinking it a difficult object, its discourses so foreign as to be almost unintelligible, and yet sufficiently enticing as to draw me into new debates and trajectories of thought I barely knew existed. When I asked one of my teachers about why there were no later issues, she told me the school had cancelled its subscription due to the magazine's "explicit content." Ten years later, this brief phrase still seems to convey the mysterious hold that *Art & Text* has always had over me.

These few volumes of *Art & Text* were to be my first experience of contemporary art, at least as I now understand it. In its texts and images, art for me became political, speculative, subjective, experimental, and, most importantly, revelatory of the opposing forces underpinning everyday life. Unlike the images I had seen in auction catalogues or deposited in state and federal galleries, the art in *Art & Text* was less about social status or codified national identity than about the world in which I lived. Despite its specialized and sometimes arcane language of cultural theory and art criticism, I could still recognize frank, if occasionally confrontational, revelations about desire, money, violence, and beauty in the magazine. Its pages offered me an extended education.

Over the years, *Art & Text* instituted a daunting program of writings that challenged readers to think about established ideas concerning not only visual art but also race, sex, and geopolitical forces. As Melbourne film and art critic Adrian Martin once observed, "Such is the gauntlet that the magazine has helped lay down: how to move through art, sometimes past it when necessary, to somewhere really significant?"[1]

From the first issue onwards, *Art & Text* introduced the Australian art world to various concepts borrowed from psychoanalysis, liberationist politics, and emerging French theory. The lessons and insights of these ideas were not always appreciated. In the Melbourne literary journal *Meanjin*, academic Stan Anson criticized the magazine's interest in recent theory, seeing it as little more than a raw bid for power: "The conservative implications of structuralism and post-structuralism have been widely remarked, and they are doubtless intuitive even to *Art & Text*."[2] It is ironic that this body of work is now widely seen as constituting an important historical breakthrough.

Founding publisher and editor Paul Taylor always maintained that art remains central to everyday life, especially noting its "practical potential" in his inaugural editorial.[3] Taylor's pragmatic critique of what he termed the "present unhealthy situation" in Australian art writing, however, could not have foreseen the looming HIV/AIDS crisis in the art world and beyond, which was soon to become the litmus test for art's commitment to cultural amelioration. Over the coming years, the magazine was unwavering in its resolve to expose this crisis.

Apart from its theoretical and street-political concerns, *Art & Text* also became a microcosm of the Australian condition. Its genesis documents an intense burst of activity by a small number of like-minded people with a vision for an entirely different kind of Australia to live in and take into the future. Much of the magazine's history can be attributed to this larger, mainly postcolonial cultural dilemma and its entrenched resistance to change. Even its coda reveals an attempt at flight from an inhospitable climate. Ultimately, *The &-Files* is a tale of over twenty years of activism in art and related ideas.

The Beginning

In early 1981, Taylor set up the office of *Art & Text* at the Prahran College of Advanced Arts, one of the more progressive art schools in Melbourne at the time. The college was situated in a fashionable and slightly alternative suburb around Chapel and High streets, an area known for artists' studios and fashion boutiques. Taylor had received a small grant from the Visual Arts Board of the Australia Council to help launch the magazine.

After graduating from Monash University in 1978 with a degree in art history, Taylor took a teaching position at the University of Tasmania in Hobart. The idea of *Art & Text* was born during his time in Hobart, and he immediately began to set up the magazine on his return to Melbourne:

> I had to do all the schlepping from scratch. I had no experience in printing and writing for a magazine, other than student rags—and a couple of articles published in magazines overseas. I had to find out about design, layout, circulation, advertising, and distribution as well as doing editorial and secretarial work, find premises and do the budgeting (and I was very bad at that sort of thing).[4]

When the first issue of the magazine came out in the fall of 1981, its masthead was printed in black text, and there was no cover image. Its serious intentions were not in doubt. Taylor's "Editorial: On Criticism" was a frank and provocative statement. He described the rival magazines then in operation—*Art Network*, *Lip*, *Art and Australia*, and *Aspect*—and argued that despite various efforts, none of these publications had developed "the foundations of a strong critical approach." There was the implicit assumption *Art & Text* would provide these foundations and so attempt to change what was possible in Australian contemporary culture. A desire to go beyond the confines of the art world in this country was clear:

> Essays by and about Australian and, sometimes, overseas artists, theoretical and cultural analyses, inquiries into the relationships between the several arts and an avoidance of extensive interviews, reviewing and lavish illustrations all aim to establish *Art & Text* as a forum for critical and artistic re-examination and experimentation. By means of such a forum, Australian artists and critics may gain a progressive understanding of their role and practical potential.[5]

To forge the new magazine, Taylor drew on sectors of the Australian art world while looking for direction from overseas currents in art and art theory. The magazine had a critical bent, but also channeled a sense of the new zeitgeist. A pool of younger artists and writers who had been sidestepped in much of late-1970s critical literature were given special support and nurturing, including Vivienne Shark LeWitt (whose name Paul had earlier suggested), Philip Brophy, Edward Colless, Maria Kozic, Imants Tillers, Peter Tyndall, and Juan Davila. At the same time, a number of new galleries, including Roslyn Oxley9 Gallery in Sydney and Arts Projects and City Gallery in Melbourne, were creating new outlets for contemporary visual art. In an interview, Taylor described his understanding of the situation that then existed:

> It was a fortunate convergence of interests in Melbourne in 1981: certain galleries, certain peripheral scenes combined together with the fact that I felt I could give some sort of intellectual stamp of approval to it all.[6]

Adrian Martin later spelled out the milieu in greater detail:

> The *Art & Text* alliance was formed under the sign of bricolage and experimentation—based more on the loose and shifting "family resemblances" between different people and their interests (whether New Wave, film theory, Australian cultural studies, specific areas within French philosophy, or any combination thereof) than a hard-and-fast "platform" with its philosophical roots deep in Wittgenstein, Saussure, Nietzsche, nominalism, idealism, fascism … (take your pick). Often pegged from a distance as "academic," the magazine in fact boasted a remarkable range of writers, from the model institutional "academic" (dogged, well-paid) to the non-, semi-, anti-, and disaffected academic.[7]

The contributors to the magazine were a diverse group. Patrick McCaughey was the founding professor of fine arts at Monash University, an art critic for the Melbourne newspaper *The Age*, and had recently completed an extensive monograph on landscape painter Fred Williams. Philip Brophy was a peripheral participant in the art world through his subcultural music/art group $\_{,}\uparrow^{\rightarrow}$ (often written as Tsk Tsk Tsk) and the Clifton Hill Community Music Centre. Janine Burke, a leading feminist art historian and active member of the feminist magazine and art collective *Lip*, had recently published the groundbreaking book *Australian Women Artists: One Hundred Years, 1840–1940* (1975) and the first monograph on the Melbourne expressionist painter Joy Hester.

Through a direct interest in his immediate Australian context, his closeness and affinity with local artists (encouraging many to write and contribute), as well as an insider sensitivity to art's overlap with music and film, Taylor helped document, guide, and create some of the more inventive characteristics of the Australian scene in the early 1980s.

Curating and Anything Goes

Around the same time as his work in *Art & Text*, Taylor also pursued a number of parallel art-world activities, the most significant of which were his anthology of Australian art writing, *Anything Goes: Art in Australia 1970–1980* (1984), and the two exhibitions *Popism* (1982) and *Tall Poppies* (1983).

Anything Goes came out shortly before Taylor moved from Melbourne to New York. It appeared under the *Art & Text* imprint and was partly financed by Roslyn and Tony Oxley. The anthology incorporates a broad range of ideas, discourses, and political interests congruent with Taylor's activities in the magazine. Reflecting his essentially freehand approach to editing, he chose to include critics with seemingly irreconcilable differences. Patrick McCaughey, who had been one of the champions of formalist art practice in Australia, appears alongside Janine Burke, an outspoken feminist and supporter of community-based art practices. The title *Anything Goes* was an astute observation about the world art in the 1970s, but it also offers great insight into Taylor's own preoccupations.

In his anthology, Taylor used different essays to illustrate core themes in the emerging art discourses of the previous decade, including,

1. The dematerialization of the art object, the commercialization of art, and sexual and racial discrimination in art.
2. The possibility or impossibility of making an interesting formalist art practice after it had become an accepted, even orthodox style.
3. The wide variety of feminist art practices and their different theories of liberation and emancipation.
4. The possible advantages or disadvantages of practicing art in Australia, an island continent with a small, isolated, and dispersed population.
5. Examples of real exchange between Australian, European, and American art worlds.
6. The ongoing influence of the Australian landscape and its attendant romanticism.
7. The rise of photography as an important medium in the fine arts.
8. Political art practice, focusing on screen-printing and posters.[8]

These declared debates or trends in art practice are readily evident in the first fifteen issues of *Art & Text* (three essays in the anthology were taken from the first issue of the magazine).[9] Acting as a prelude to his own future ambitions, the final contribution to *Anything Goes* was Taylor's "Australian 'New Wave' and the 'Second Degree'," in which he proposed a unique style of Australian postmodernism. By this simple gesture, he boldly attempted to position himself as heir apparent to all manners of art and critical taste in Australia at the time. As if to vindicate his bravura and innate self-confidence, fate somehow succeeded in turning Taylor's theoretical prophecies into historical fact.

Two years before publishing *Anything Goes*, and only one year after founding *Art & Text*, Taylor put together his *Popism* exhibition for the National Gallery of Victoria. Featuring the work of Howard Arkley, David Chesworth, Ian Cox, Juan Davila, Richard Dunn, Paul Fletcher, Maria Kozic, Robert Rooney, Jane Stevenson, The Society for Other Photography, Imants Tillers, Peter Tyndall, and Jenny Watson, *Popism* was marked by a self-conscious plea for what we now term postmodernism. It was followed in 1983 by *Tall Poppies* at Melbourne University Art Gallery, which featured the work of John Dunkley-Smith, Dale Frank, John Nixon, Mike Parr, and Imants Tillers. Revealing an important aspect of Taylor's curatorial method, *Tall Poppies* selected artists on the basis of a common theme while also enhancing their visibility in the art world. This approach is further evidenced by the Imants Tillers exhibition he curated (along with Sydney gallery owner Kerry Crowley) for the Australian Pavilion at the 1986 Venice Biennale.

The Early Issues

Contributions to the first fifteen issues of *Art & Text*, of which Taylor was sole editor, were principally from Australian art writers and scholars, but there was also a range of overseas offerings, mainly in translation. Perhaps the most famous of these were Jean Baudrillard's "The Precession of Simulacra," translated by Paul Foss and Paul Patton, in *Art & Text* 11 (Spring 1983), and an interview between Roland Barthes and Bernard-Henri Lévy, translated by Stephen Mueke, which appeared in No. 8 (Summer 1982–83). Perhaps as significant for the dissemination of new critical theory in Australia, however, was Philip Brophy's first-issue review of Dick Hebdige's *Subculture: The Meaning of Style* (1979).

Taylor was a society figure in the Melbourne scene, fraternizing with artists and other members of the art world and holding parties at his apartment in South Yarra. This led to the appearance of "page works" (artist projects designed for print), critical manifestos, and short statements by some of the more interesting artists at the time, among them John Nixon's "Manifesto for a Renewed Art Practice 1980" and Peter Tyndall's "Culture Corner" (both in No. 2, Winter 1981), Vivienne Shark LeWitt's "Why Egyptian Mods Didn't Bother to Bleach Their Hair, or More Notes about Parkas and Combs" (No. 3, Spring 1981), Juan Davila's "Spider Woman in Australia" and "Spider Woman in *Playing with Fire!*" (No. 4, Summer 1981), and a number of seminal pieces by Imants Tillers, Lyndal Jones, John Young, and the collective Zerox Dreamflesh.

Taylor's last issue before moving to New York was a collaborative effort with the British magazine *ZG*.[10] Founded by Rosetta Brooks at the very end of the 1970s, *ZG* had tried to expand the traditional scope of an art magazine, bringing together essays on music, fashion, and politics. This desire for a broader "cultural" focus resonated with Taylor's editorial agenda for *Art & Text*. After setting up in New York, however, Taylor completed one more issue of the magazine, another joint effort with the Canadian magazine *File*, first launched in Toronto in 1972 by General Idea (AA Bronson, Felix Partz, and Jorge Zontal). The *File* joint issue, with its fanzine attitude toward pop culture, cultural theory, and gay politics, is perhaps the clearest realization of Taylor's desire for an international amalgamation of art, theory, and pop culture. Similar attitudes can be found in Sylvère Lotringer's *Semiotext(e)* magazine and monographs (1974–), Thomas Lawson and Susan Morgan's *Real Life* (1979–94), as well as Rosalind Krauss and Annette Michelson's *October* (1976–).

Among the various innovations to be found in Taylor's early issues of *Art & Text* (as well as those achieved later by editor Paul Foss) is the generally understated larger cultural appeal of art. As Adrian Martin puts it in his "Before and After *Art & Text*," "The story concerns not only the life and death of a special cultural moment, but the general state of art culture—the function of magazines, the role of 'theory.' The use of expanded discussion lifting from art."[11] What Martin points to here is magazine production as the self-conscious engine of art-making and criticism, and the insistence that art plays an important role in the overall direction of contemporary life.

New York and Paul Foss

By 1984, Taylor was keen to find someone to take over as full-time manager of the magazine. He asked Melbourne artist and critic Robert Rooney and then the Sydney writer George Alexander, but both declined. Paul Foss, whose first contribution to *Art & Text* was "Meridian of Apathy" (No. 6, Winter 1982), agreed to assume the role, allowing Taylor the freedom to pursue his ambitions in New York. Toward the end of 1984, Taylor left Melbourne, and Foss was installed in the South Yarra apartment-cum-office to run the magazine. Although Taylor continued as co-editor for a time, the bulk of his commitment to the magazine now lay behind him.

In New York, Taylor's successes were many. He wrote widely on many key figures like Andy Warhol and Robert Mapplethorpe, curated an important exhibition on Malcolm McLaren (New Museum, 1988), and discoursed extensively on art, money, and influence—much of it posthumously documented in an anthology organized by Foss, *After Andy: SoHo in the Eighties* (1995). In the second half of the 1980s, Taylor was diagnosed with HIV. After a decline in his health in 1992, he returned to Melbourne. He spent his last days in the Royal Melbourne Hospital. His obituary in *The New York Times*, dated September 22, 1992, reads as follows:

> Paul Taylor, an Australian art critic, journalist and editor known for his championing of popular culture and his critical profiles of art world personalities, died yesterday at the Royal Melbourne Hospital in Melbourne, Australia. He was 35 years old and had lived in Manhattan from 1984 until this month, when he returned to Melbourne.
>
> Mr. Taylor died of AIDS-related lymphoma, said his companion David E. Johnson of Manhattan.
>
> A native of Melbourne, Mr. Taylor graduated from Monash University there in 1979, and quickly established himself as a force in Australian art circles, writing on contemporary art for several Australian magazines and newspapers.
>
> In 1981 he founded the magazine *Art & Text*, which became the first Australian journal to achieve an international readership.
>
> After moving to New York City, he worked primarily as a freelance journalist, writing on the art scene for *The New York Times*, *Vanity Fair*, *New York Connoisseur*, *Flash Art* and *The Village Voice*, among others. In 1988 he organized the exhibition "Impresario: Malcolm McLaren and the British New Wave" at the New Museum of Contemporary Art in Soho.
>
> Besides Mr. Johnson, Mr. Taylor is survived by his mother and stepfather, Patricia and Charles Edward Bartels, and two brothers, Gregory and Philip, of Melbourne.

April 2008

1. Adrian Martin, "Before and After *Art & Text*," in *What Is Appropriation?*, ed. Rex Butler (Brisbane/Sydney: Institute of Modern Art/Power Publications, 1996), 116.
2. "On Being Difficult: The Conservatism of *Art & Text*," *Meanjin* 42/2 (1983), 213.
3. "Editorial: On Criticism," *Art & Text* 1 (1981), 11.
4. Imants Tillers and Paul Taylor, "Images and Words," *Follow Me (Gentleman)* (June/August 1986), 99.
5. "Editorial: On Criticism," 11.
6. Ibid.
7. Adrian Martin, 109.
8. (1) Ian Burn, "The 1960s: Crisis and Aftermath," in *Anything Goes: Art in Australia 1970–1980*, ed. Paul Taylor (Melbourne: Art & Text, 1984), 8–25. (2) Patrick McCaughey, "Ten Australians," ibid., 30–45. (3) Ann Stephen, "A Process of De-neutralizing" ibid., 62–67; and Janine Burke, "Sense & Sensibility: Women's Art & Feminist Criticism," ibid., 116–121. (4) Terry Smith, "The Provincialism Problem", 46–53, and Paul Taylor, "Australian New Wave and the 'Second Degree'," ibid., 158–167. (5) Daniel Thomas, "Art and Life: The Actuality of Sculpture," ibid., 98–107. (6) Robert Lindsay, "Relics & Rituals," ibid., 108–115. (7) Christine Godden, "Photography in the Australian Art Scene," ibid., 132–143. (8) Julie Ewington, "Political Postering," ibid., 88–97.
9. That is: Ian Burn, "The 1960s: Crisis and Aftermath"; Janine Burke, "Collaboration: Artists Working Collectively," ibid, 122–131; and Paul Taylor, "Australian New Wave and the 'Second Degree'."
10. See "Zines for a Day: Matthew Higgs on the Other Art Press," *Artforum* (March 2003) for an introduction to *ZG* magazine.
11. Adrian Martin, 115.

1. Torsos in a Publisher's Gallery

An Open Letter from Paul Foss

Robert McKenzie
Melbourne
Australia

December 22, 2007

Dear Robert,

It has been exactly two years since you first approached me about an interview concerning my role in ART & TEXT. As you know, I was reluctant in the beginning because I am averse to publicity of any sort, including seeing my name in print. It's not because I am shy or particularly standoffish, but has more to do with what I believe are the real philosophical drawbacks of introspection and every attempt at accountability. Most of the time, I'd prefer to leave discussion of my work to others.

But my aversion runs deeper than that, complicated by people's misunderstanding of what it is that publishing editors actually do. Much of my adult work has gone into the pages of ART & TEXT, and, more recently, ARTUS, yet somehow it remains traceless because of the nature of the beast. It's useless to protest. Pointing out the extent of my editorial input into a diverse range of writings, even sometimes going so far as ghosting them or authoring work under assumed names, tends to come across as vain and curmudgeonly, despite all the acknowledged work I have penned over the years. I've generally had no option but to keep the illusion going, if only because that's what one is supposed to do.

Then your offer arrived, and I realized I didn't feel particularly comfortable talking shop. The main issue for me wasn't so much to do with dredging up acceptable answers, but shielding myself from the risk of sentiment or a false sense of propriety, because unless questions are aimed at third-person events or actions, one is caught in the same motivational bind. Walter Benjamin expresses this dilemma admirably in a 1932 fragment called "Excavation and Memory," in which he notes, "for authentic memories, it is far less important that the investigator report on them than that he mark, quite precisely, the site where he gained possession of them."

Faced with this renewed demand for authenticity, and to protect myself from the crazy ideas people have always harbored about me and the magazine, I concluded that I, too, as Benjamin goes on to say, must "return again and again to the same matter; to scatter it as one scatters earth, to turn it over as one turns over soil. That is to say, [to] yield those images that, severed from all earlier associations, reside as treasures in the sober room of our later insights—like torsos in a collector's gallery." Somehow thinking of the task in these terms, as an autopsy on the corpse of my own memories, made it more bearable.

I'm not sure whether what follows is up to the task I have set for myself. But it will be understood if I continue to examine the confusion of my own history with the history of the creature that has nevertheless long dominated it. I trust the two are not identical, but it is naturally difficult for me to bring about a total separation. Did I create the magazine, or did the magazine create me? Are we both the accidental product of a revolution in time, with the result that neither of us can be pulled asunder? Dipping into the archive again, Benjamin's "Note for On the Concept of History" (ca. 1940) sheds light on this confusion: "Marx says that revolutions are the locomotives of history. But perhaps it is quite different. Perhaps revolutions are what happen when the humanity traveling in this train snatches at the emergency brake."

Let me be just as blunt. Every attempt at APOLOGIA implies as much self-justification as self-documentation. In truth, digging into one's past entails a lot of arduous spadework. The terrain varies enormously, requiring different tools to meet the task at hand. But no matter what trade one plies, all who have had the questionable luck to participate in tumultuous events, if they care for the advancement of the greater good, ought to treat the story of their own life as a form of historical critique, even though they should not venture on such a "splendid undertaking" (Cellini) without also recognizing the often very human refusal to act in time.

Nowhere is this indecisiveness clearer than in my own life. I grew up in Marrickville, an industrial inner suburb of Sydney. In my teens, I built a laboratory in the backyard and carried out experiments. I once knew Partington's book on inorganic chemistry by heart. I soon enrolled in a pharmacy course at the University of Sydney, eventually receiving a master's degree in pharmacology. After this, I worked for four years at the University of Wisconsin-Madison, where I helped develop the commercial manufacture of L-dopamine used in the treatment of Parkinson's disease.

At Madison I was also involved in discovering a new class of prostaglandins, those naturally occurring lipid compounds sometimes used in childbirth. I visited a local abattoir once a week and stuck my hands into the freshly slaughtered cattle to remove their still-writhing prostate glands. I will always remember the sight and smell of all that blood and the roar of the workers' radios above the mêlée.

During my time at Madison, I learned to operate a mass spectrometer. An extremely important tool for molecular analysis, this complicated instrument also produces the most wonderful visual diagrams or blueprints. I've always felt a rough-and-ready comparison can be drawn between technical editing and the interpretation of mass spectrographs, which essentially reduce given molecules to measurable wave functions. Even back then, I thought these drawings would make excellent artworks. It has taken the art world many years to accept scientific diagrams as a form of valid expression.

In August 1970, the Weathermen blew up the University of Wisconsin's Sterling Hall, killing a physicist and injuring four others. I was working in another part of the building earlier the same evening and easily could have been hurt. This period of American history now seems conveniently forgotten. Over the previous year and a half there were 4,330 bombings across the country, causing at least 40 deaths and 384 injuries. At Madison, I witnessed army tanks rumbling down campus streets, people being dragged around by their hair, gassed, arrested, and other terrible things. The demonstrations took place in front of the very laboratories where military and other sensitive research continued unabated, as if the turmoil outside had been merely a student prank. It was all very disturbing and led to a personal epiphany of sorts, for up to that point I had never paid any mind to world events.

Suddenly, everything turned upside down. Armed insurrection in the streets didn't help.

Eventually I ended up back at the Australian National University in Canberra, where I began research in marine biochemistry. But laboratory research was never quite the same again, so I rather precipitately enrolled in a doctoral program in history and philosophy of science at the University of New South Wales, where I ended up teaching for a number of years. It was time well spent, as this implicitly revolutionary discipline serves to bridge the hard sciences and humanities, reminding us of the profound relativity of all received truths.

Not unrelated, perhaps, to all this schooling in science and philosophy was my longtime fascination with experimental writing and publishing—activities that began for me with a few satirical pieces for student magazines. But at some point, this literary interest overtook the more scientific one, insofar as I became more intrigued with critical philosophy. The road that the history of science had opened up for me led straight to the French historians of medicine, such as Foucault and Canguilhem, and from these figures to the whole structuralist and post-structuralist debate, into which I soon threw all my efforts. This is how my interest in translation work also began.

In the late 1970s and early '80s, I was heavily involved in a semi-underground scene involving liberation movements of every stripe. I gave a paper titled "Theatrum Nondum Cognitorum" in 1981 at the inaugural semiotics conference in Sydney, which more or less sealed my fate as far as giving up academic life was concerned. After that, I became more involved in cultural production. I was researcher on a 1982 mainstream Australian film called KITTY AND THE BAGMAN *and dabbled a bit in television documentaries.*

In 1983, Sylvère Lotringer at Columbia University approached me about publishing a translation I'd done (with Paul Patton) of Jean Baudrillard's "The Precession of Simulacra," which not long after appeared in Lotringer's SEMIOTEXT(E) *series of monographs. This translation was quickly followed by* IN THE SHADOW OF THE SILENT MAJORITIES *the same year. I can't recall the precise motivation behind these and other translations from around that time, but they may have been intended for a forthcoming Feral publication series, which already included* LANGUAGE, SEXUALITY & SUBVERSION *(1978) and* MICHEL FOUCAULT: POWER, TRUTH, STRATEGY *(1979)—one of the first English anthologies of its kind.*

There is a funny but equally sad story about this entirely community-produced series of books. They were funded mainly by a wonderful gay man named Terry Bell, now deceased, from his liaisons with a famously closeted senator in Australia (whom I well remember pacing anxiously up and down outside our Randwick apartment). Thanks to this misadventure, we got to influence the local critical scene and even the direction of discussion at universities.

I eventually ran into Paul Taylor, who was a recent fine-arts graduate from Monash University in Melbourne. He had attended the Sydney University semiotics conference and heard my paper. He wanted it for ART & TEXT, *which he launched later the same year. But the essay was already committed. Paul often credited this conference as the inspiration for* ART & TEXT, *though on other occasions he pointed sagaciously to* OCTOBER.

Being older and, I hope, more experienced, I didn't really take to Paul at first. He was anxious to go to New York to work as a critic for important magazines, which, miraculously, he pulled off. One can get a good idea of what Paul went on to accomplish by looking at his anthology of critical writing, AFTER ANDY: SOHO IN THE EIGHTIES *(1995), which I helped* organize after he died. It contains his main New York essays, except for the one in which he gossiped about the famous critic and historian Barbara Rose. She was so incensed that she slapped Paul's face at a public forum, so I didn't want to take any chances.

In 1984, Paul started looking around for someone to run ART & TEXT after he moved to New York, and I seemed to be the only person even vaguely interested—not surprisingly, since it was not a real paid job. But I was somewhat flattered to be asked, so I agreed to do it for at least a year. That year eventually stretched out to 2002, when the magazine and I finally parted ways.

Even though Paul's interest in ART & TEXT waned after he began to make his mark in New York, during which time the magazine came ever more under my control, I grew to like Paul enormously, and we saw a lot of each other. He was very charming and great fun to be around, but he was also a horrid tease. Whether hollering out to passing trade along Fifth Avenue or soliciting prostitutes in Puerto Rico, you always had to keep a close eye on him.

When Paul grew ill, he and I became very close—or I felt we did. As the disease progressed, he faced all of that in a remarkably brave way. I would never have imagined it. When we traveled to Documenta IX in 1992, I had to carry his wasted body onto the train. Some embraced him and others turned away, but he didn't complain once. It was devastating to watch him die. When I tried to put together some New York obits to publish in ART & TEXT, the legendary Leo Castelli wrote a short eulogy, but Roberta Smith of THE NEW YORK TIMES copped out, even though she was Paul's friend and promised me she would. It saddens me to think that anyone could be so heartless.

Paul initially wanted me to bring the magazine to New York, but I remained ambivalent. I had already been bitten once in the U.S., and so shied away from the idea. Now I think I should have followed his advice. But starting with the magazine's relocation from Melbourne to Sydney in 1986, and then the long, slow haul of moving offshore culminating in 1999, the inevitable attraction of moving overseas drew me back to the original crime scene.

This was not a decision to be made lightly. The magazine received substantial, long-term support from the Australian government, and I had a free hand in just about every department. For almost two decades, ART & TEXT had been perceived as a regional publication with international appeal, but now I wanted to push this idea to the limit. I also wanted to improve my own editorial skills—I needed to be more in the swim of things if I were to continue publishing.

I first met Susan Kandel in 1995 on the advice of Amelia Jones and John Welchman, whom I already knew from when he taught in Melbourne. At this time, Susan was a critic at the L.A. TIMES and taught occasionally at Art Center. We soon hit it off and started to discuss her getting more involved in the magazine. Susan was a naturally gifted writer and personality in her own right, so it seemed like a good idea. I was probably not thinking clearly—editing an art magazine is often less exciting or rewarding than most people bargain for. In retrospect, the decision to go ahead seems inseparable from my eagerness to pass on the magazine to someone else.

The initial proposal was to set up an offshore base in Los Angeles, but I soon grew tired of all the travel involved and decided to move there permanently. The year 1999 was a watershed in recent Australian history, when it seemed the country's political and cultural prospects under the conservative leadership of John Howard were never going to improve.

I thought it was time for me to leave, little imagining the cataclysmic events I would soon encounter in the U.S. The magazine, meanwhile, went ahead with increasing its size and developing a new design concept.

By the beginning of 2001, I realized that Susan wouldn't be staying the course, so I needed to come up with another plan. Around the same time, I learned I was ill and probably wouldn't be able to continue doing the magazine. I didn't know what to do. Funds started to dry up, as I never obtained the same level of support in California as the magazine had once enjoyed in Australia. I thought of returning home, but a reluctance to abandon my earlier resolve to stay prevented me from carrying it through.

Understandably frustrated with constantly battling the clock to meet deadlines, and overwhelmed by the shock of finding myself ill in a country without a public health system, I just stopped doing the magazine. There wasn't much more to it than that. So many of my friends and colleagues had already been taken by this disease—Terry Bell, Paul Taylor, Eric Michaels (whose remarkable AIDS diary, UNBECOMING, I first published in 1990), and my dear friend Julian Omen who helped me with the magazine for ten or more years—and now it seemed my time had come as well.

After almost a year of complete rest, I gradually pulled myself together. I missed working on the magazine, but I no longer had the energy to do it on such a grand scale. This is how the germ of ARTUS took hold. I'd always wanted to explore other possibilities in art publishing, so my having survived this recent setback seemed like an excellent time to begin. Indeed, I grabbed at the fate of being in a country facing a crisis of its own.

The new magazine was originally supposed to have been a team effort, but most of that proved illusory. I soon found myself back where I had begun almost twenty years ago, more or less on my own. It got my dander up to leave things as they lay. Yet even if the venture had failed as an exercise in group therapy, it quickly changed tack into more familiar territory, where once again events conspired to help develop new critical languages in response to the times. It's funny how things work out. ARTUS ended up being not so different from its earlier incarnation, after all.

At this precise moment, it is hard to say how much longer I can continue down this path. I'd like to think I could move on if I wanted to, but I confess to remaining just as curious today about where the current scene is heading as I was all those years ago. This is ultimately why I decided to talk about myself in this fashion. You have kindly taken the step of asking me why, emboldening me in turn to believe that somehow the time was not wasted.

Yours sincerely,

Paul Foss
Los Angeles

2. Producing the Line

Paul Foss interviewed by Rob McKenzie

ROB MCKENZIE: **Your first issue of *Art & Text* was called "Burnout" (No. 16, Summer 1984). Why did you choose to start there?**

PAUL FOSS: It was 1984, so referring to George Orwell's book seemed in order. I suggested "Burnout" as an appropriate warning against postmodernist theory turning into a form of Newspeak. Paul Taylor in turn was obsessed with the difference between fame and glory, arguing that the latter was clearly superior, yet he wasn't beyond stealing someone else's thunder if it suited his purposes. So the cover line also worked as a cheeky caveat to Paul's ambition.

Taylor had offered the editorship of the magazine to a number of other people before he offered it to you, and you were hesitant to accept. Why was this?

Because I realized that it would be all work and no pay. I didn't trust the situation and knew I would inevitably be left holding the bag, which is what happened. If I hadn't joined the magazine, though, I would never have got to know Paul and all the other people and places I've encountered over the years, so it was the right decision in the long run.

As your background was outside of art—in chemistry, political activism, and philosophy—how did you feel about taking over the editorship of what was ostensibly an art magazine?

I don't think I ever thought about it in that way. To my mind, it was just another way to secure a stake in intellectual life. What probably mattered more was my background in publishing—which extends from my student days to the present—as well as my having a working familiarity with recent theoretical developments. I've always had broad interests, so doing an art magazine was no special leap for me. Anyway, I like a challenge.

In the late 1970s, you worked with Meaghan Morris and Paul Patton on the *Working Papers* series. Can you talk about the circumstances surrounding these publications?

Meaghan and I worked on the two Feral books—*Language, Sexuality & Subversion* (1978) and *Michel Foucault: Power, Truth, Strategy* (1979)—and the earlier *Working Papers* series devoted to sexual theory. But many people were involved in these radical endeavors, so it's not correct to attribute them to any single person or core group. It was in fact Terry Bell, now deceased, who was the driving force behind these publications. Terry deserves pride of place in the history of queer Australia.

I've never seen the earlier issues of *Working Papers*.

And nor would you, as they're now lost among the dust of minor history. I think I have kept everything, including various prototypes such as *Gay Liberation Press*. You should check out Fisher Library at the University of Sydney.

Was *Working Papers* a continuation of work started with *Gay Liberation Press*?

The seven or so issues of *Gay Liberation Press* started out, more or less, as a radical homosexual zine serving the immediate Glebe area, whereas *Working Papers* (produced by much the same team of people) represented a larger, more Situationist style of address. The latter project eventually led to the two Feral publications. A third book was planned, supposedly on revolution and desire, but somehow it never happened.

The third book was to have been titled "The Philosophy of Desire," and include a translation of Deleuze and Guattari's *Rhizome* (1976). How much of that book was ever completed?

Very little, I recall. By the early 1980s, the dream of permanent revolution had pretty much dissipated. People split and went their own ways—mostly into academia, the art world, Qantas Airways, you name it. But our *Rhizome* translation finally ended up in *I&C* magazine (London).

The Feral books published translations and discussions of the then relatively unknown Michel Foucault, Luce Irigaray, and Umberto Eco. How did you come across these figures?

Most of the Sydney people involved with Feral were graduate students or scholars in one form or another, so we all had fairly diverse interests and contacts.

Did you obtain these texts from the countries in which they were published, or did you come across them in Australia?

Some I came across in a French bookstore in New Caledonia! The world seemed smaller then, with Sydney having far closer ties to Toronto, London, Paris, and New York than it has today. I had the benefit of inhabiting this particular crossroads. People talked and I tended to listen.

Meaghan Morris studied in France during the early 1970s, so was she a key point of contact?

In those days, Meaghan always seemed to play her cards pretty close to her chest. She's a formidable intellect. When she and I first met in her backyard in Glebe in the mid-1970s, she was stark naked. I don't think she was ever really the committee type.

What was it, then, that attracted you to these new discourses?

The interest in Foucault came directly from my research in the history and philosophy of science, although by that time many people either knew about or had read *Les Mots et les choses*. I recall seeing the 1966 Gallimard edition sitting prominently on Meaghan's mantelpiece one day, and when I inquired she confessed it was her bible and that just looking at it calmed her—or words to that effect. As for the Italian connection, certainly George Alexander, who was a student then in the Italian Department at Sydney University, was among the earliest in Australia to bring attention to Umberto Eco and Jean Baudrillard (via Italian translations). And Liz Grosz was, and is, a major Lacan expert.

When did you start doing translations?

I dabbled in European languages at high school and university—where I took a class in scientific German with one of Einstein's secretaries (or so they said). But I'm a self-taught linguist, more debutant than diva. That still didn't prevent me from throwing myself into "the task of the translator," as Walter Benjamin once prosaically described it, and I quickly got hooked. It's great fun being stuck in between two languages, yet somehow emerging with a serviceable compromise or two. This idea of having to let something go in order to preserve the overall flow of the argument has very much influenced my editing practice.

Like editing, translation is a form of production with low visibility. Was this an aspect of its appeal?

I don't think translators could be said to have low visibility. Many names have been forged on the anvil of translations, from Erasmus and Luther all the way through most of the important post-war German and French philosophers and writers. Even in my own infinitesimal case, it's only because of the translation of Baudrillard's "The Precession of Simulacra" that my name is known at all, certainly in the U.S. Baudrillard, by the way, began as a translator.

So how do you account for this preoccupation?

I don't know what the appeal is. Ultimately, my translation work has never been a simple act of communication, or about staking a theoretical claim by proxy (however much this may be true in other circumstances), but has functioned more or less as random thought experiments in, shall we say, the task of writing. Yet irrespective of whether the task concerns editing or translating, sometimes there indeed occurs something like an out-of-body experience, which I suppose might be considered a kind of invisibility.

The translation of "The Precession of Simulacra" appeared in *Simulations* **(1983), the first monograph in Semiotext(e)'s Foreign Agents Series. How did you come to work on this translation?**

I independently roughed out a first draft and then passed it on to Paul Patton, who edited it. Around this time, I was reading Pierre Klossowski and may have been drawn to Baudrillard because of the simulacrum connection. Regardless, Sylvère Lotringer used it to launch his new venture. Now in its umpteenth printing, today the little black book seems a bit out of its time, much like the series itself. But these monographs made an important intervention in the 1980s and should be recognized as such.

Had you circulated this translation widely?

I don't exactly know how people found out about it. It appeared first—or simultaneously, I can't remember which—in *Art & Text* 11 (Spring 1983), Paul having badgered it out of me. Had I drawn his attention to it, or did he know about it beforehand? In any event, its Australian publication caused quite a stir in the local cultural scene, because that's when things started to heat up in institutional debate, and even young artists got into the act. One result of this sea change was the art spoof *Art & a Texta* that started appearing in Sydney bookshops, a fringe publication Paul had the temerity to sue.

Did you ever meet Baudrillard in person?

Patton and I interviewed him once on public radio. Baudrillard eventually became a cult figure in Australia, attracting unprecedented crowds at his Sydney University lecture a few years after "Precession" came out. He was a sensitive, almost whimsical man, though he looked remarkably like a greengrocer. In my estimation, Baudrillard helped to neutralize the art world's reliance on the dialectic of "good" vs. "bad," so he should probably be considered in the same company as Greenberg.

During the late 1970s and early '80s, before you took on the editorship of *Art & Text***, you were a freelance intellectual. Is that an accurate description?**

After leaving the University of New South Wales, I traveled for a time overseas and on my return worked in film and television and other odd jobs. But throughout this period I continued writing and translating. I didn't have any special plans. Then Paul came along and dragged me to Melbourne.

Were you aware of *Art & Text* **before you met Paul Taylor?**

I doubt it, but somehow Paul knew all about me. We may even have crossed paths at the 1981 Foreign Bodies conference at Sydney University, where I delivered a paper.

I definitely recall running into him once in the company of George Alexander in a gay bar on Oxford Street—I can't say absolutely when. Paul once told me the idea for the magazine came from that semiotics conference, but I don't believe a word of it. My name first appears as a contributor in *Art & Text* 6 (Winter 1982), so I must have been aware of the magazine by then.

Can you remember your impressions of the magazine before you took on the role of editor?

Not really, but consider the circumstances. Paul was only in his twenties when he launched *Art & Text* not long after a short teaching stint in Hobart. He had in mind something akin to an antipodean *October*, which he was very familiar with. He was determined to broker his way into the New York critical scene, so the theoretical reach did make sense for that time and place. I don't know the extent to which Paul could be said to have crafted these early issues out of whole cloth, not as I understand it at least. He never discussed his editorial philosophy with me.

There seems to be an overlap between *Art & Text* and publications like *October* and *Semiotext(e)*, as well as *ZG* and *File*, with which there were joint issues (Nos. 15 and 22 respectively). Was this the context you saw for the magazine?

I was not involved in organizing those double issues, although they both contain contributions from me. What strikes me about them now is that they clearly reveal the general direction of Paul's publishing ambitions on the eve of his newfound freedom. His *ZG* editorial, "How a D.J. Saved My Life"—an appeal to the new arts as so many "cover version[s], in the tradition of Saint Veronica's veil"—notably suggests the path he would have traveled if circumstances had decreed otherwise. We can glimpse something of this new direction in Paul's New York monographs and catalogue essays, but to my knowledge he never again worked on an art magazine after the *ZG* double issue.

Had Paul ever discussed with you what the magazine was supposed to be about?

If he did, I don't remember it. But I wasn't thinking very far into the future then. This is why I had no particular agenda for how I was to proceed in the wake of Paul's departure.

So you had no notion at all about what doing this magazine would entail?

My background is in empirical research and scientific philosophy, so I have a knack for observing and abstracting data. I also welcomed the opportunity to think about how to present images and words on the printed page, which is perhaps not dissimilar to interpreting the molecular workings of a mass spectrometer, in which I was once trained.

One would think that you needed a better orientation to the task than these more arcane skills.

But I had no intention of doing the magazine for more than a year. I may have entertained the thought of injecting a little more order and rigor into its content, but that is where it ended.

Did you explain this to Paul?

Paul was hard to pin down in those days, and I still wonder whether his proposal to "share" the magazine with me was anything more than a lark. I suspect I wasn't too serious about it, either. Due perhaps to our natural bond, he and I never talked about anything very practical other than in a casual manner. And given his enormous personal charm and sharp wit, this badinage became all the more irresistible to me. He was great fun, yet clearly uninterested in staying the course past a certain stage.

Some people have suggested that you both immediately fell out over the magazine and tried to cover it up.

I think I may have intimidated Paul a bit in the beginning. The day before he died in Melbourne, Paul said some very kind things to me. I treasure those comments, so I would never repeat them.

Were you critical of him in the early days?

Many people were critical of Paul back then, which he didn't deserve. I liked him—I just didn't trust him. To me he was capable of anything.

What was he criticized for?

When Paul left Australia, he was roundly accused of using the magazine as a calling card to New York, but that wasn't fair. It seems unlikely the infant magazine would have opened many doors that actually mattered, so I think we should give him credit where credit is due.

It may have been because he was so much younger than most of the major players in the Australian art world at that time.

I think it had more to do with the sheer cheek of the guy. Besides, he might have had to tone down his rhetoric at first after a less-than-enthusiastic response to the magazine in New York, confirming for him just how much he needed me to stay in the picture.

What are you suggesting?

That he rapidly came to see that together we could take the magazine further than it had reached so far. I'm only guessing, of course.

Did you want that level of involvement from him?

I basically wanted out. But Paul intrigued me. His greatest strength as both a person and an editor lay in his ability to remind you of some offhand remark you had once made, as if he was always listening to you. Listening is a very rare skill, as is its constant companion, bringing people together.

Did you respect him more as a person or as an editor?

In my experience, communicating and intellectualizing are not the same thing, so your question is unanswerable. Though, of course, the art of editing doesn't lend itself to general accord. I have known many first-class writers who seem to draw back when it involves editing the work of others, as if they were desecrating holy ground. Paul was no exception. His style of editing was a fairly relaxed one, and not at all what is sometimes considered interventionist, which is what I am mainly accused of. Paul's approach was to hold a dinner party and then leave everyone to clean up the mess. All of that was a bit frustrating at first, but I just kept a low profile.

There were plenty of other publications in Australia around this time, including *Agenda*, *Tension*, *Local Consumption*, and smaller zines like *Xerox Dreamflesh*. As well, you must have been looking at various underground or academic publications from which you took your inspiration. Nothing can exist in a vacuum.

As a rule, a drop in pressure generates hurricanes. So it is with magazines too. I don't think it particularly helps praising them to the skies, since magazines are by definition occasional and incomplete—as the French term *hebdomadaire* still manages to denote, pointing to their ecclesiastical origin. As a rotating weekly roster for singing mass and generally leading in the saying of prayers, the hebdomadal tone of many magazines depresses me. There never seems to be any end to them, especially in today's online proliferation. This may be why my early *Art & Text* issues appear like bolts from the blue, whatever their faults.

Would you say your attitude toward the publications that appeared around the same time as *Art & Text* was one of exclusion?

Perhaps a whiff of indifference, but it is not at all exclusion. It was simply a procedural caution, especially as I see no reason to enlist others to account for my own failings.

You moved from Sydney to Melbourne in 1984 to take up the role of co-editor and production manager of *Art & Text*. Going on the magazine imprint, up till that point the publication seems to have been a one-man band.

Although Paul had a very loyal following of friends and supporters.

Can you describe the atmosphere at the magazine when you first took over?

At that time, Paul had an upper-floor apartment in a smart deco building near the river in South Yarra, renting a space on the ground floor for his poolside office. My arrival there must have been around late August, because I remember Paul surprising me with a rent boy for my birthday, which I can't say exactly thrilled me. It was obviously a planned maneuver to win me over to whatever bad news was to come. He did, however, reveal remarkably good taste. As it turned out, Chris ended up living with me for most of the time I was in Melbourne.

I heard that you and Paul had a fight over your refusal to send his gift away.

Something like that occurred at the airport when Paul flew out. I just said that if I'm to clean up his bloody mess, then I obviously need help. He wisely let the matter drop.

How were the reins transferred?

On my arrival, Paul and I began moving the office upstairs to his apartment, where I was to live and produce the magazine in his absence. It offered a very fine view of the Yarra basin, so I didn't mind. But what did give me cause for concern was the revelation that the magazine would have to meet Paul's mortgage payments while he was living in New York, presumably in exchange for my room and board. When I mentioned to him that this probably wasn't prudent, he laughingly cited as precedent how a well-known Melbourne artist had recently bought a horse farm with his Australia Council grant. I knew instantly it was a mistake.

How did you handle this thorny affair?

Paul always struck me as the Jewish princess type. He was not a bad person or anything like that, yet he clearly had issues. I knew he was very attached to his mother, Pat Bartels, who doted on him to the extreme. Prior to my arrival, Pat and Paul had come up with a rough budget for the next twelve months, but it didn't hold water. Far more worrying was the news that we needed to cover Paul's living expenses in New York, whether through new government grants or increased advertising. I got the impression that Paul thought I had influence in higher circles, which was hilarious under the circumstances. It soon became clear that the magazine was a tissue of wishful thinking, which was not an auspicious beginning.

Yet you chose to stay.

There are no easy answers as to why I decided to remain in Melbourne, other than to say it wasn't immediately convenient for me to return to Sydney. Things turned surreal when Paul duly informed me that I also had to oversee the distribution of his newly published anthology, *Anything Goes: Art in Australia 1970–1980* (1984). That really tore it. That's how matters stood when Paul flew out of Melbourne a week or so later.

Did you finally distribute *Anything Goes*?

Yes, and much more besides. But I don't want to give the impression that I thought any the less of Paul because of this or any of the other snafus he threw my way. He liked to test how far people could be pushed. He soon learned, however, that I needed a realistic plan in order to fall into line, and if one did not present itself, then I would come up with my own.

The magazine must have proved a difficult financial exercise.

It was, but no more so than I expected. I was mainly annoyed with Paul's unreality principle about fundraising, something of which I had no experience whatsoever. I knew enough to realize it was crucial to keep the books straight, and that the money had to be visible on the page and not in the pad. Paul's idea of accounting was to stuff all the receipts, bank statements, and invoices in a shopping bag and take them to his mother's old accountant, who, as it turned out, went bankrupt himself. Many of the people I have known in the art world have proved hopeless at fundraising, myself included.

On a not-unrelated topic, while still in Melbourne you published a special issue called "Phantasm and Simulacra: The Drawings of Pierre Klossowski" (No. 18, July 1985). How did this come about?

I think I'd gone to New York that year and met Allen S. Weiss, who was one of Annette Michelson's students. This special issue was entirely Allen's idea, although I contributed a little footnote on certain reservations I had about Klossowski's "laws of hospitality." The great philosopher even replied to my piece in a letter he wrote me afterwards, which remains one of my cherished possessions. Allen basically chose everything, and we shared or farmed out the translation load. For some reason, Paul insisted his name be included as one of the editors of the issue, which was lame as he had had nothing to do with it. I found it a bit hard to take Paul seriously past that point. This standoff between us probably lasted for two or more years, during which time we grew more distant.

Like Paul Taylor, Allen S. Weiss was based in New York. He later worked on the "Art Brut" issue (No. 27, December 1987–February 1988) and then as a contributing editor. Did he provide an alternative to Paul's influence?

Don't forget Allen also edited and organized the "Nonsense" supplement in No. 37 (September 1990), which occurred in conjunction with the Whitney Museum.

Was Paul "involved" with this issue, too?

Paul didn't care about the magazine by this stage, but I don't generally think about intellectual life in terms of direct influence. Human beings are more polymorphous than that. In any case, others don't really "influence" me so much as offer paths of mutual intrigue. I've always admired the discipline and rigor that goes into Allen's writing, but it doesn't extend much further than that, nor do I feel he would necessarily think it should. And this goes double for Paul. The only influence I can ever imagine him having over me would have occurred "under the influence."

Nonetheless, it is hard to imagine the magazine without their input.

Of course, both Allen and Paul left their mark on the magazine in quite different and very considerable ways, but that doesn't mean I automatically agreed with everything they did, or that I couldn't have done without them. It's hard explaining what people like me precisely do.

Do you mean publishers, or editors?

The term *publisher* doesn't quite apply in my instance, and even though I've always assumed the position of editor come what may, that won't do, either. It is compounded by the fact that here we're not discussing the accepted profession, but something quite out of the ordinary and maybe even a little dangerous. Publishing editor comes closest, but if pressed, I prefer the term *line producer*.

Can you explain this term?

It's simply a film metaphor applied to another industry renowned for mystification and hyperbole. It also neatly covers all the deadlines and demands that our stressful job entails. In this context, the line producer would be responsible for producing the "line" of the magazine, which involves normal editing and the magazine's appearance, but, more importantly, for preserving the overall integrity of the enterprise.

That doesn't sound so different from how magazines are usually described.

It's not so dissimilar on the surface. The main difference arises at the level of performance. For any magazine, large or small, the task entails juggling a lot of people, ideas, and material limitations. The immediate goal may concern getting out an issue or selling advertising space, but none of that is possible unless everyone is kept in line, laying the groundwork for future collaborations. That has very little to do with the public face or *mysterium* of the art press, which hopefully a concept like line producer is able to avoid.

Are you recommending a new division of labor or consolidation of standard editorial practice?

I'm not even going that far. What I am proposing instead is a little different, which is that a phrase like *producing the line* helps us understand precisely what magazines do and, at the same time, don't acknowledge they do, giving appearance to the line at the expense of its disappearance—the line as a simultaneous negation of what it prescribes.

Can you be more specific?

Simply put, we know the verb produce means to make appear or draw forth something that is hidden. Magazines are a production in this strict sense, except they can't show whatever they like, not if they are to reach a target audience or sell advertising. So a line has to be drawn somewhere, some limit on how far they are prepared to go, but which can never be revealed as such. The line of the magazine is everything it feels constrained to limit itself to without giving this limitation away. So whoever is in charge of production has to be a kind of magician, palming off as tricks what must forever remain a secret.

Could this metaphor also be applied to what you have tried to do?

Absolutely, except, in my case, I can't resist drawing attention to the underlying magic act.

The final issue you published out of Melbourne was Nelly Richard's "Margins and Institutions: Art in Chile Since 1973" (No. 21, May–July 1986), which in many ways is more like a book than a magazine. Nelly Richard first contributed to *Art & Text* 8 (Summer 1982–83) with a Juan Davila interview. What is the backstory to the "Margins" issue?

It was a true labor of love—and semi-fiasco. I'd already had a taste of Nelly's demanding prose style when working with a professional translator on her "Notes Towards a (Critical) Re-evaluation of the Critique of the Avant-Garde" (No. 16, Summer 1984–85). This time, I thought the translation would run more smoothly if I worked directly with her closest friend and ally, Juan Davila, a Chilean artist who had resided in Melbourne since the coup of 1973. Juan, who was really the conduit for all of Nelly's contributions to the magazine, came around to the new office in Kensington every day for weeks on end to work on the text with me, sparking many intense discussions about the sorts of cuts I deemed necessary for the English context, not least because it was supposed to be a bilingual publication. I gather Nelly was none too happy with the result.

Do you mean the translation or the whole issue?

A bit of both, perhaps. Back then I still used the traditional cut-and-paste layout system, based on copy produced by an old Brother word processor. During Nelly's issue the keyboard broke, and I had to type out her entire text using replacement keys for certain malfunctioning letters. Proofing presented many predicaments, requiring a lot of hand pasting at the last moment. It's a miracle that issue ever saw the light of day, all the more so since it was the first time contemporary Chilean art had been discussed at length in English. The other day I heard the book is being republished in Chile, probably with a new translation.

It sounds like the line of production broke here.

Yet *Margins and Institutions* conjures up many fond memories for me, mainly to do with the office I rented after convincing Paul that funding his South Yarra residence was hardly appropriate. Close by the office was a leafy park, where Juan and I took lunch every day during our sessions. At my prompting, Juan even photographed a young lad who regularly tended the gardens. Working with Juan was a terrific experience, not least because he has a very wicked streak. He is very important to the history of the magazine. He convinced Ian Howard (then director of the old College of Fine Arts in Paddington) to provide office space for the magazine when I moved it to Sydney.

Davila was a frequent contributor to early issues of *Art & Text*, beginning with "Spider Woman in Australia" and the photo spread "Spider Woman in *Playing With Fire!*" (No. 4, Summer 1981). More significant, perhaps, is Juan's involvement in other publications linked to the magazine. For instance, the 1985 monograph *Juan Davila: Hysterical Tears* includes an interview by you with the artist and an essay by Nelly Richard, though Paul Taylor is solely credited as editor. What was the story there?

I think Juan was very appreciative of my efforts toward his first monograph. This is another example of how Paul liked to keep everyone occupied, but hogged the limelight. I didn't really care. Bylines have never mattered much to me, only all the steps leading up to them.

Weren't there other collaborations between you and Juan?

Juan was the principal benefactor and co-conspirator of another publishing venture of ours, the Art & Criticism Monograph Series. The first monograph in this series was the collaborative *The Mutilated Pieta* (1985), in which I replied to a painting of Juan's. Juan and I penned *Pages from Maria Kozic's Book* (1987) under the name Danielle Duval. Maria wasn't too happy about it, however. Artists assume different personas in their work all the time, but somehow writers must always be themselves.

Was this series about the role of agency in art writing?

Well, there's Allen S. Weiss's solo text *Iconology and Perversion* (1988) and Eric Michaels's *For a Cultural Future: Francis Jupurrurla Makes TV at Yuendumu* (1987), which is one of the most important documents I ever published. Juan and I had no presence here at all. That said, Juan's earlier essay, "Aboriginality: A Lugubrious Game" (*Art & Text* 23/24, March–May 1987), casts an entirely different light on agency in Eric's text today.

Eric Michaels is another pivotal contributor, a young American anthropologist who had come to Australia to work with indigenous communities. His first article appeared in the same issue as the Davila piece you just mentioned. How did you become aware of Eric's writing?

Meaghan Morris first spotted Eric. She caught his keynote address at the Australian Screen Studies Association Conference in Sydney (in December 1986) and suggested it for publication in the magazine, as she was a contributing editor then. This introduction led to a short but very productive association between Eric and me, continuing well after his death from HIV/AIDS in Brisbane in August 1988. You already mentioned "Aboriginal Content: Who's Got It—Who Needs It?", which was quickly followed by "My Essay on Postmodernity" (No. 25, June–August 1987) and "Bad Aboriginal Art" (No. 28, March–May 1988). These last two are definitely some of the best essays the magazine ever printed. I think Meaghan especially admired the Madonna piece, teaching it in some of her university classes. "Bad Aboriginal Art" is now considered a classic. It ended up as the title essay of his posthumous anthology, *Bad Aboriginal Art: Tradition, Media, and Technological Horizons* (1994), which I later edited and helped organize. Finally, through a series of bureaucratic blunders at the height of the AIDS hysteria, Eric ended up dying in Australia intestate, even stateless.

Tell us about Eric's state of mind in these trying circumstances.

Eric was one of the people I most admired during my time at the magazine. You only have to read his caveat on the back cover of the "Bad Aboriginal Art" issue to get a sense of the sheer chutzpah of the guy—he bitch-slapped tribal provincialism and its ties to the emerging Aboriginal art market. It took real guts in those days to defy elder authority from inside the left, which is what running "his" photograph of the tagged Yuendumu doors effectively did. I was very nervous about running this image on the front cover, but went ahead regardless. It is perhaps one of the greatest risks I've ever taken as a publisher, far more so than the ones showing semi-naked boys or the man masturbating.

Did you discuss the risks with Eric?

He left it to me to decide, but we were not close friends. When Eric became ill, I visited him twice in Brisbane. He seemed alienated from his immediate family, so I felt obliged to go. Even though he had a number of academic allies close by— mainly the anthropologist John von Sturmer and photographer Penny Taylor—Eric clearly needed gay people around him. Death and dying really freak me out, so I was worse than useless. In order to appear on top of things, I suggested he might keep a diary of his experiences. We rarely spoke about it afterwards, but when he subsequently died and I looked in his laptop, to my astonishment I discovered a fully realized account of the last year of his life, which was eventually published as *Unbecoming: An AIDS Diary*. Such documents are rare in professional life. Eric left behind the most beautiful gift any human being can bequeath his own kind, which is probably why the diary has continued to attract serious scholarship ever since. What is truly remarkable is that I hardly knew the guy, having only met him under professional circumstances.

Although going by his account of your reactions to his illness in *Unbecoming*, you must have been devastated when he died.

Death before one's accepted use-by date always elicits the most frantic reactions. When Eric succumbed, his double status as a foreign national and a forensic risk to public health meant he was quickly cremated. Somehow this did not dissuade his American parents from seeking to obtain his ashes for the purpose of giving him a proper burial back home. Going against Eric's express wish as noted in the diary, his executrix Penny and I decided the ashes should be delivered to his parents after all, mainly because we thought they also had a right to bury their undead. I didn't think this was a betrayal. For us, Eric will live forever through *Unbecoming*.

Although, it is sad he didn't get to have the last say.

Obviously, no one was prepared for death on this scale. I'd arranged to hand over the urn to Eric's parents at Paul's apartment in New York, but I didn't alert him to it beforehand. When I arrived from the airport, I put the urn on his mantelpiece and said, "Paul, I'd like to introduce you to Eric." He was mortified. My only excuse is that no one knew then who would be next.

You have said that Paul Taylor wanted to relocate the magazine to New York, but you didn't go along with the idea. At the end of 1986, though, when you moved back to Sydney, you took the magazine with you. What can you recall now of those machinations?

This was the age before emails and cheap overseas calls, so I used to write Paul long, conspiratorial letters from Melbourne, which rarely received a reply. Any pros and cons about moving the magazine to New York would have been hammered out in those letters, which Paul apparently destroyed in 1992 when his declining health forced him to clear out his apartment and return to Melbourne. But there's no mystery as to why I felt disinclined to duke it out in the mean streets of Manhattan.

I imagine you are referring to the belief that the magazine couldn't compete there in its current form.

On the other hand, I doubt Paul had much interest in the magazine after I took it to Sydney. He clearly didn't want this to happen, but it also seemed to absolve him of all further responsibility. As for me, I was always looking to pass it on to someone else. But somehow the magazine stuck, as a viable alternative never seemed to present itself. I had hoped that moving it to COFA might help find it an academic home, but that never happened either. For years, various people came and went, but nothing ever changed. It soon became evident that unless I figured out a plan to abandon ship, I'd be chained to it forever. So I started considering how I could drastically limit my involvement, figuring—not surprisingly—that if the magazine counted for anything at all, I wouldn't even have to face this dilemma.

Around this time, I notice you began to expand the magazine's staff, beginning with a new managing editor.

People were always inquiring about some job or other, but they were never realistic about what it would entail, and they never lasted very long. It is depressing watching pipe dreams evaporate, especially since no one ever believed you when you told them it would happen. It has always frustrated me no end, because I don't ever recall thinking an art magazine would be a walk in the park, especially in this tiny neck of the woods. It suggests a storybook attachment to losing your way in a dark forest, which in other circumstances wouldn't be tolerated. You'd think that any child of the media age would be able to see through such a fantasy.

That's a tough nut to swallow. You, of all people, would have to know that production and reception are always means to the same end, so understanding one from the point of view of the other requires some prior, often privileged knowledge.

That is exactly the sort of fairytale I mean. Whether or not production and reception have the same apparent aim, that in no way diminishes the fantasy of fame and fortune that always lingers just beneath the surface. I have no idea why these myths prevail. I doubt anyone serious about writing or publishing thinks like that, doing it mainly out of duty. And publishing criticism in earnest is a bit like undergoing a surgical procedure without anesthetic, so you really have to have nerves of steel in this business.

I am only suggesting that we shouldn't confuse these matters at the level of production.

As I've already suggested, production already encompasses this level of confusion. Take art writing itself, which, in my experience, attracts numerous people of varying ability. Of those who go so far as to submit articles to magazines, a lot of them are nonetheless shocked to discover their efforts might need resuscitation, even down to obvious mistakes. They soon learn that they either have to forgo getting their own way or give up all hope of writing.

I now understand why you have a reputation for being a very tough editor.

I know writers don't want to hear it. A contributor once complained to me that I obviously expected people to be better than they are, which is the best feedback I ever received as an editor. A good editor knows how to recognize these mystical projections in the scene of writing.

Writers also think that editors have prearranged and mostly arbitrary agendas they then get subjected to.

The myth of editorial detachment is ultimately just as regressive as the myth of literary freedom, both of which constitute a distraction from more practical concerns. But editors passionately need writers, just as writers technically need editors. It is a kind of pas de deux where both parties are caught in a mutually beneficial embrace. And just as the writer has to come round to learning how to dance, so must the editor be prepared to follow his or her lead. So long as editing and writing are understood in this way, then what shows through is a type of group dynamic or therapy.

In No. 26 (September–November 1987), there is an article by Jean-François Lyotard and Jacob Rogozinski titled "The Thought Police," addressing a number of criticisms of French post-structuralism by younger French writers, but whose broader terms clearly rebuke the negative criticism then directed by Australian commentators at so-called French theory. What was the response like for you?

Ideas are not tied to any individual or group, and "French theory" is no exception. Even the term is posthumous, evoking as it does a life it never actually had. It is nonetheless true that something like Adorno's "vain commotion of unfreedom" rapidly settled over the whole affair and on either side. Foucault, for instance, was roundly critiqued along old lines of empiricism versus rationalism or was the brunt of ridiculous claims about the lineage of fascist thought in twentieth-century philosophy, while more zealous partisans took cover under universalizing redactions.

Including yourself, it would appear, going by the title of *Michel Foucault: Power, Truth, Strategy*.

Point taken, but look at what happened in the meantime. For some of us, leaving the academy seemed the only solution, even though people like Liz Grosz and Paul Patton stuck around and tried to make a go of it. This was ultimately not about the real critical work being carried out in Paris or Sydney but the larger cultural changes occurring everywhere in the world during this period. Smallish magazines like *Art & Text* were caught in the backwash of these tidal fluctuations, but the main turbulence occurred upstream.

Robyn Stacey's *Nowhere to Go* photograph on the cover of No. 26 is particularly poignant given the scenario you describe.

That issue provides a fairly accurate snapshot of the state of the art world in Australia at the time. Instead of politely ignoring or underplaying the situation, those voices already in the air were given the opportunity to make a discreet appearance, leaving the object of their critique open (for example, the broken discourses surrounding HIV/AIDS).

Although the magazine afterwards began to move away from an engagement with theory per se, you clearly maintained an interest in the *realpolitik* that drove these speculative texts. This is evident right up until the present, even in the material you are now publishing in *artUS*.

It's not correct to say that after a certain time *Art & Text* moved away from theory. Times changed, as did the nature of theory. A different kind of rhetoric and radical lifestyle emerged. One would hope that the very idea of presenting radical ideas in the language of traditional or academic systems of thought had begun to lose its appeal after a while, and as a consequence people started to invent new, more instantaneous languages. That, at least, is how I view the history of this era, as a series of abrupt gear changes.

I imagine you are referring to the period leading up to the fall of the Berlin Wall and the first outbreak of hostilities in Iraq.

The late 1980s and early '90s is certainly when the discussion in the news media took a sudden U-turn to the right, so much so that it became virtually impossible to mount a critique from opposite points of view, let alone suggest the possibility of real opposition. This was the ugly side of postmodernism, whose consequences we are still living with today. But the language of criticism can no more take the moral high ground of world events than be ground to dust beneath them, and in this regard is inseparable from what Gaston Bachelard once described as the "reinforcement of what peeks out from behind the appearances" (*Le Nouvel esprit scientifique*, 1934).

How can art writing achieve a critical stance and still remain relevant to art?

Perhaps one should revisit Bachelard's concept of "la phénoménotechnique," which proposes that scientific theories, rather than provide models of relative verisimilitude, act more like machines for producing phenomena under reproducible conditions—a noumenology that segues neatly into Foucault and Deleuze's "toolbox." There is indeed a certain parallel with taking critical theories out for a spin, seeing where the conclusions might lead. For me, the great advantage of the art world is that it offers a blank slate for doing almost anything, from behavioral science and happenings all the way through to collective insanity—not that blank slates are ever neutral, but it's a start.

The early issues in which you were involved are also notable for their commentary on HIV/AIDS. In No. 17 ("Expositionism," April 1985) you published "The Challenge of Loss" by Sam Schoenbaum and then "Body Fluids" by Didier Gille and Isabelle Stengers in No. 26. These seem to be significant interventions in the troubled discourses surrounding the topics of risk and infection.

"Expositionism"—which, by the way, is one of my favorite issues—was co-edited by Paul and me. Sam was Paul's Australian friend in New York, so "The Challenge of Loss" was entirely his suggestion. As for "Body Fluids," I came across it in an issue of *L'Autre journal* that Sydney curator Judy Annear brought back from Paris for me, so the translation is simply an example of serendipity.

Far more telling perhaps is the self-referential aspect of this issue, where all the images are moved up the front into an "Iconographies" section.

This is a tactic aimed at that historical moment in time, in which we see a mock Frankfurt School horror of spectacle literally in bed with the standard Brian De Palma image of voyeurism. But I don't think anyone got it.

The inclusion of the HIV/AIDS material was understandable given the total crisis everyone was expecting then.

Especially with the recent surfacing of Paul's suspicions about his own situation (in those days, diagnosis was mainly guesswork). But our tactic was somewhat different from the approach taken by the emerging ACT UP movement. Paul was the product of a later generation when direct action was no longer a priority, and I realized appealing to the public conscience was never going to work.

Did you both feel that a more intuitive, performative line of attack was required?

That pretty much sums up the content in "The 'Thing' " issue (No. 20, February–April 1986), which contains Boyd MacDonald's "Art from the Post-Heterosexual Age," interviews with Allen Jones and Gilbert & George, and Duncan Smith's analysis of Levi's 501s and The Saint (the infamous New York sex club and viral watering hole). The cover even flaunts Gilbert & George's *Ass* (1980)—I've forgotten whose it is now. Paul would know.

A lot of criticism was leveled at the magazine's level of sexual—particularly homosexual—content.

It may seem incredible today, but back then there was a concerted effort in the art world to silence the discussion of HIV/AIDS, especially by many so-called feminists and assorted lefties who paradoxically ended up as the worst kind of bigots. The few rude covers seemed to cause the most offense, as if these were the only things that people ever looked at.

How do you approach cover design?

I've always been interested in the technical limits of cover design. My covers especially are rarely what they seem. Take *L'Ombre luxurieuse* on the cover of the Klossowski issue (No. 18): was showing it a "blatant act of sexism," as some whispered back then, or was it an attempt to hold up a mirror to acts of misdirected homophobia? Some very cruel things were said in those days. It's important to know that some people then even said gay men deserved to catch AIDS. They are still saying it.

In a recent discussion a colleague commented that "we are all concerned firstly with our own bodies." This raises an important issue, I think. Have your publications been informed by what might be understood as a political commitment to subjectivity?

No publication is worth anything more than its immediate circle of correspondents, either in the form of contributors or as readers, so subjectivity is the nature of the beast. In my opinion, reducing subjectivity to a preoccupation with "our own bodies" is mistaken.

So what was the magazine's underlying agenda toward the politics of self?

I can't speak for Paul, but my commitment was to have no commitment—at least to anything fixed or sewn up. It is the readers who bring their own thoughts or desires to the table, while leaving the best of intentions on the side. It's all in the detail, in unfettered access to the spread from every angle or inclination. Given my background, I can't see it any other way.

Is this belief related to the collapse of the "master discourses" during the 1980s?

Yet what collapsed also bounced back twice as insidious. One might generally trace the history of critical subjectivity during this period as beginning in the late 1970s with the breakdown of hard-line, communist-style rhetoric, then the surfacing of momentary perestroika in the early 1990s, followed by the recent cracks in autonomous world government, and ending in the McDonaldization of global identities. That story makes an appearance from time to time in the magazine, but not the bland endorsement of subjectivity as such.

And naturally, people get quite annoyed when they are forced to look at something they don't particularly like.

This question of bias is quite unanswerable, as is trying to pin down the actions one invariably takes. There are always so many reasons for *not* doing something that, by the time everything comes together in the final object, one's personal preferences would seem the least of it. If I truly had in mind the kind of magazine some people have claimed, I would never have done what you see now. Given everything I've written or published over the years, it's hard to believe that anyone would think differently of me.

So you don't think that homosexuality and subjectivity are thematically or strategically related?

My comments only refer to those very few issues Paul and I happened to edit together, which, alongside his *ZG* and *File* joint issues and my later "The AIDS Crisis is not Over" (No. 38, January 1991), are among the queerest of the whole collection. But look at the essay I contributed to No. 38 ("The Children's Crusade"), which deals with the news media's obsession with child abuse and its link to state terror. What perhaps makes these issues of *Art & Text* still hold up today is their reluctance to toe the line on questions like sexuality and subjectivity, which is the very opposite of how they were seen.

What were the major developments and stages in the history of the magazine?

I'd like to hear what you think. I only saw the magazine from the inside, which is not exactly "history."

The first stage, 1981–84, was when Paul was in charge (Nos. 1–15). The second was 1984–86, the time you spent in Melbourne (Nos. 16–21). The third corresponds to 1986–91, the period devoted to re-establishing a base for the magazine in Sydney (Nos. 23/24–38). Following that, in 1991–96, you attempted to build up the magazine's international profile (Nos. 39–55). The years 1996–99 saw the gradual consolidation of the Los Angeles connection (Nos. 56–66). Lastly comes the relocation to the U.S. in 1999–2002 (Nos. 67–78).

There is, of course, a seventh phase, that of the magazine's re-emergence as *artUS*, beginning in 2003.

There are, however, overlapping strands of a more internal nature. For example, you introduced a section of exhibition reviews in the magazine from No. 28 onwards. How did this come about?

By that time, I'd become restless and started to put out feelers. Part of me wanted to ditch the magazine entirely. Another part was genuinely interested in developing alternatives to the art magazine format.

And yet you made certain concessions to tradition.

Constantly tinkering with the process seems to be part of my method. Each issue suggests a new set of technical problems to which future issues are then devoted, problems that only get worked out at the level of new material, raising, in turn, an entirely different set of problems, and so on. Much of this had little to do with readymade arguments or political goals, which I only ever loosely connect with, but more the idea of viewing material through the lens of production, and not the reverse.

Does this mean you didn't so much introduce a reviews section for the reviews themselves but as a way of testing the editorial process?

That's one way of putting it. Of course, reviews are an unavoidable fact of art publishing. Even the traditional feature is a kind of extended review.

But did you feel compelled to give more emphasis to reviews to silence the opposition?

I suspect that somewhere in the back of my mind was a growing fascination with what it is that draws people to reviews more than anything else. Is it only because they are quick and easy to read? And what makes criticism different from the academic essay? From an editor's perspective, editing reviews usually involves much more labor and skill than your average feature. This all began to add up in my mind.

Does the short attention span required by reviews irritate you?

Yet it's instructive how the topic of writing always comes down to a question of length or substance. Articles are either too short or too long, too light or too heavy, but in the meantime no one is attending to the established systems of legibility on which these judgments are based. Drawing attention to the given limitations or technologies of art writing is an ongoing preoccupation of mine. In this respect, an art magazine doesn't have to be about art or the art world at all. It could actually be a concerted effort to return all opinion to ground zero.

After you returned to Sydney in 1986, the magazine seemed to exist in a state of flux until 1991, when "The AIDS Crisis is not Over" (No. 38, January 1991) and "Zones of Love" (No. 40, September 1991) special issues appeared. Had you been searching for a way to make the magazine more viable, or was it a question of acclimatizing to the new surroundings?

To me, it's a bit like that scene in the film *Gattaca* where Ethan Hawke's character discusses swimming out so far from shore that it would be pointless turning back, as one would surely drown anyway.

Another fairytale analogy, although this time you are the would-be hero.

I've taken many personal and economic risks during my time at the magazine, not that anyone was generally made aware of it. It was even the case that I grew increasingly despondent over whether it was worth continuing at all. I suppose I'm a word junky when all is said and done, so to me the magazine has always assumed the dimensions of a clandestine hobby, something to be kept very close to my chest while rarely bothering to inquire why. I really am to blame for this costly obsession of mine.

And were those two issues I mentioned the point at which prospects began to improve?

It's funny, because "The AIDS Crisis is not Over" was to have been the magazine's swansong. The opportunity first presented itself in the form of interviews left over from a BBC documentary organized by Simon Watney, although I tried to introduce responses and artworks from Australia as well. I thought if the magazine closed down afterwards, then at least I'd done something useful. Ironically, it was this issue that turned everything around for the magazine. Australia Council funding increased substantially after that.

Was "Zones of Love" already in the works?

I'm not sure now. "Zones of Love" seems to have been about investigating other forms of sponsorship, given the Japanese supplement's tie-in with Judy Annear's exhibition at the Museum of Contemporary Art in Sydney, the commercial gallery backing for the Stelarc spread, as well as the presence of lots of advertising and—I believe—the first major appearance of color.

What kept you going during the previous five years?

When I returned to Sydney, I immediately started looking around for alternatives. I was already doing the monograph series with Juan, and I also agreed to put together an anthology of recent criticism for the forthcoming Australian Bicentenary, *Island in the Stream: Myths of Place in Australian Culture* (1988). The magazine only paid me expenses, so I was forced to look elsewhere for income. I even tried editing other people's doctoral theses. But the magazine somehow stuck fast, like a creature of my own making. It was more through luck than anything that it ever got as far as No. 41 (January 1992), at which time the magazine took off in a new direction.

Before you moved the magazine to Sydney, you must have reflected on the necessity of obtaining long-term government funding. How do you understand the intersection of state interests with your own publishing activities?

It's actually highly compromising, like being paid for services rendered. But it would be naïve to think that one is able to do without some level of executive privilege in the world of fine art. As a feudal system, art has it all over Big Brother.

I heard your new relationship with the Australia Council was difficult at first.

Around the time of the move, I met with Ross Wolfe, then director of the Visual Arts Board, to discuss the double issue (No. 23/24, March–May 1987) I deemed necessary to arrange hauling everything back to Sydney. I had explained this to Ross in an earlier phone conversation, but he later denied it ever took place and grew testy. Our discussion became heated, until I realized my protests could be heard echoing throughout the whole building. Going by the look on Ross's face, I must have been a sight to behold.

What happened to the funding for that issue?

Nothing more was ever said about it. This was only a minor incident in a long and fruitful partnership, even if I haven't always agreed with some of the Australia Council policies.

You mean their basic policy toward funding international art magazines?

It's all part and parcel of the same dilemma. Australia's relatively isolated position vis-à-vis the global market has all sorts of consequences, so extra effort needs to be made by government departments charged with ensuring the country's cultural future. After 1983, when the Labor Party came to power under the leadership of Bob Hawke, Australia Council policy rapidly expanded the export of local culture as a direct arm of foreign policy, which basically meant reducing the arts and crafts to the same level as wheat or weaponry. But the idea of importing the action to our shores seemed to elude everyone. That would have entailed having real hands-on experience, which in turn would have meant accepting art as a market-driven exercise and not some budding league of nations. The tidal flow of world art is indifferent to individual shorelines.

Is this really due to Australia's geographical isolation or an exaggerated sense of self-reliance?

I imagine our collective mythology and Canberra are equally to blame. So long as governments adhere to the international biennale format as a universal barometer of cultural success, then the risk always remains that the alleged benefits of this policy will flow outwards rather than inwards, the prevention of which is surely the reason for subsidy in the first place. I don't want to overstate the case, as no one has benefited more from Australia Council policy than myself.

What did you do to circumvent or challenge this policy?

From the get-go, I realized that accepting government grants under these circumstances only reinforced the cultural vacuum that the system was allegedly charged with eliminating, laying the foundation for unavoidable collisions further down the track. Obviously, these are not things one can easily discuss with bureaucrats. My only recourse was to stop applying for grants, which is what I did eventually.

Was there a particular grievance with the Australia Council that led to this?

One thing I did complain about was the quota system applied to Aboriginal and non-Aboriginal content in funded magazines. As *Art & Text* dealt more or less exclusively with contemporary art, the system was unworkable. There are a few young Aboriginal artists, but that still didn't prevent the policy from being counterproductive or even discriminatory. When I tried to say as much, the only advice I received was simply to fudge the facts.

Given what a lot of the material in the magazine had already tried to say, you must have found this situation exasperating.

It's not that I am unrealistic about how bureaucracies work. In many other respects, the Australia Council and state-funding bodies have made great strides in helping to create more opportunities for Australian artists in the overseas context. This includes helping some of the more contemporary galleries with their freight costs to international art fairs.

Do you think this outweighs the more questionable aspects you just described?

My argument is that branding art along national lines cannot remain the final word. Like it or not, Australia is a small country with no particular economic or strategic significance in the postmillennial age. It once had considerable import in those arenas, and may yet do so again, but I don't think one can claim that Australia has meanwhile become a major cultural destination—unlike, say, China or even Cuba. Of course, I'm only seeing this from a distance.

Living in the U.S. probably gives one a jaundiced view of Australia's national image.

The real question is nevertheless the limited market for much of Australian contemporary art. I stand to be corrected, but I don't think one could say that the bulk of the trafficking in American or European art is restricted to those regions alone. And this is not just about mass or "local spirit" but the aerial lift of a product line disencumbered by unnecessary state baggage.

Don't you think that the situation has changed because of the Internet and cheaper airfares?

What is far more important is that quite culturally diverse peoples are now moving around the globe at an unprecedented rate. The very notion of cultural identity has become ever more restricted to legal and biogenetic determinations, making the concept of national autonomy a fairytale at best. Peripheral cultures can only eke out a generic existence in today's global market.

How do commercial galleries figure in this process?

Generally speaking, galleries operate outside the demand for local representation. A lot of galleries show art from other countries, and rarely does this have anything to do with "internationalism" or "global exchange." Contrary to many museums and the like, which remain indebted to regional or local corporate interests for their main funding, galleries tend to take a more risky approach, often looking to cash in on the latest trends among private collectors, who now potentially live anywhere in the virtual world.

So what you're saying is that the standard, nationally based policy of cultural funding doesn't address the contemporary reality.

Not exactly: it does address the reality, but this is still in the mold of those merchant princes of old who used splashy art and architecture as covers for more covert military or monocultural purposes. I think the time has come to let our paintings go.

Since we're talking splash, in the early 1990s *Art & Text* saw a marked increase in advertising.

Well, ads are not just about money. Like most people in this business, I am fascinated with advertising and everything that goes along with it. It's the same with TV. I far prefer the ads to the normal programming, because here you are taken to the real world of contemporary culture, where all the lies, terror, and manipulation are there for everyone to see. So an art magazine made up entirely of advertising would seem pretty ideal to me. Then at least it would be consistent.

Is this because you're not at all interested in doing an art magazine of this sort?

I rely on the hope that the art magazine brief is sufficiently broad to encompass just about anything. What I think the inexorable rise of advertising culture underscores today is a reciprocal flight from the temporal and intellectual demands of reading, replacing the long slow digestion of illusory hard facts with the indomitable quick fix. This is not to say that one has a real choice anymore. As in "The Emperor's New Clothes," not even the child's revelation at the end of the story stops the royal procession in its tracks.

It seems clear that few people in today's art world follow criticism closely, other than as a form of publicity.

And art critics are mainly a quarrelsome lot who are best kept out of the way of collectors, who are far more concerned with word of mouth than the language of criticism per se. This is the everyday conundrum faced by the editor or gallery owner. For a magazine to proceed otherwise requires a fundamental rethink of the whole culture of publishing.

In the present climate, it becomes increasingly difficult to avoid making editorial content the servant of advertising.

There's something to be said for the way Le Corbusier approached the dilemma of advertising in *L'Esprit nouveau* during the 1920s, which involved soliciting brochures from manufacturers and then inserting images from them into printed articles, attracting a hefty bill from the publisher. His tactic neatly circumscribes publicity as such, turning it into a form of cultural seduction.

The opposite line of attack would hopefully aim for something less Machiavellian. But that still doesn't address the rule of advertising in most art magazines.

The irony is that art magazines would secretly be better off without advertising. It constantly confounds and yet projects the power of art, and so becomes all the more distracting.

In *Art & Text*, there seems to have been a number of explicit strategies for placing advertisements.

And more generally with how those strategies might connect up with the treatment of images themselves. Having to incorporate set designs within your own prescribed layout is a fiddly and always compromising process, especially when the distinction between commerce and opinion must be preserved. Le Corbusier's tactic becomes all the more fascinating in that regard.

Did you attempt to separate advertising sales from editorial duties?

I stopped having much to do with advertising after a while, leaving it to others. Although I do recall being called in from time to time to settle disputes.

So running a lot of advertising was a completely neutral act according to you?

Nothing is ever "saved" through publishing. My only objection to Madison Avenue is that its fascination comes at a price, mainly by affording the product's afterglow too much value. However, there are lots of opposing instances. Ads designed and paid for by artists can sometimes act as a counter-irritant, such as Linda Benglis's 1974 *Artforum* ad. Too bad publications like that no longer exist.

The Sydney gallery owners Roslyn and Tony Oxley in particular supported the magazine at crucial times in its history. What did this mean for you personally?

Roslyn and Tony belong to a small handful of people in Australia who have worked hard to promote international contemporary art. They've also taken Australian art overseas and brought it wider recognition. The support they gave Paul Taylor in the early years was not only admirable but, as things turned out, far-sighted. Their interest in the magazine never wavered over the twenty-something years of its existence, and that has meant far more to me than any advertising account.

The commercial gallery scene is fascinating, but some see this as its curse.

It is certainly tougher than it looks, given the inherent wickedness of artists and the havoc they are always causing. This makes for some pretty amazing individuals, who most days have to tread carefully around bruised egos and impossible demands. Commercial galleries are the grand spectacle of the art world, the worst and the very best of it. They comprise the central stage on which art parades its never-ending story, creating scenes and changing costumes at will. Yet it is a vertiginous form of fascination, since the drama always leaves one anticipating the fall.

Publishing a magazine like *Art & Text* must have brought you into contact with a lot of gallery owners and staff.

These are relationships fraught with ambivalence, because naturally magazines are always looking for advertising, and galleries of course want coverage. The two desires are not often reciprocated. The needs of artists are not necessarily the same as the needs of galleries, nor does the critical stance of magazines exactly instill confidence. It's like the modern relationship, a mix of saving appearances and still getting a piece of the action.

In the late 1980s and early '90s the magazine underwent many changes, not least being the move to full color, lots of advertising, a larger format, and offshore printing. What fueled this drive to take the magazine to the next level?

It's both revealing and depressing to hear you laying out the trajectory as bluntly as that, especially since I never planned for any of it to occur.

Yet you obviously made a concerted effort to move forward.

To me, it always seemed circumstances drove the magazine rather than the other way round. For instance, much of its mature style and appearance (beginning with No. 56, February–April 1997) derived from an impulse call I once made to the editor of a Sydney fashion magazine, from whom I got the idea of printing in Korea. He suggested I could have a much better product for a lot less money. I even flew to Seoul to check out printers for myself.

Did anyone at the Australia Council make a comment about outsourcing?

Outsourcing wasn't an issue in those days. But it turned out that printing in Korea was crucial for global distribution, providing a central departure point for moving shipments quickly to Europe, North America, and Australia. It certainly instilled in me the need to work to strict deadlines, as well as introducing me to the world of customs agents and freight companies. I find this sort of everyday stuff fascinating, but also exhausting.

Are you still printing in Korea?

I've worked with the same Korean printer now for more than ten years, Winston Park. I suspect I might not have continued publishing as long as I have if it weren't for Winston.

What about the move to color?

Excluding covers and prime advertising, color first started appearing regularly with the "Nonsense" issue (No. 37, September 1990). It's funny to reflect now on why this seemed like such a big deal back then. I remember Peter Townsend, the founding editor of *Art Monthly Australia*, once remarking at a public forum in Sydney that black-and-white is an inescapable aesthetic and political choice, as color inevitably buys into spectacle and all the consumerist claptrap—which is ridiculous, but that's what people said in those days. Meanwhile, I notice *Art Monthly Australia* has long since gone full color.

Color's association with commerce and class prestige now seems to have gone by the board.

In fact, color may be one of the main barometers of revolutionary change. Behind all of it there lies shadows and perceptual aberration.

Didn't you once argue against using color?

I like both color and black-and-white, although it all depends on how and where they are used. Nowadays, with five-colour laser printing and the growing presence of iPods and phone cameras everywhere, the game has completely changed. It's funny now to reflect on Goethe's claim that light is "the simplest, most undivided and most homogenous being that we know. Confronting it is the darkness." For instance: "Yellow is a light which has been dampened by darkness; blue is a darkness weakened by the light" (*Theory of Colors*, 1810).

Are these changes part of the downside of postmodernism you implied earlier?

This story has certainly yet to receive the attention it deserves. In the early 1980s, with Reaganomics, emerging globalization, and a booming art market, many people in the art world seemed to forget their earlier principles and dove headlong into the festivities. Here you could find every character imaginable—former Maoists, old libertarians, recovering heroin addicts, society dames, newspaper hacks, and even big government—flushed with new talk of "clients" and "accountability." One of my fondest memories from those years is when Meaghan Morris, who had been a key figure of the left in Sydney, jokingly told me she would run from one end of Bundeena Beach to the other for five bucks. But I was never sure if she meant it.

In the case of *Art & Text*, the allure of halcyon days also seemed to persevere long after their use-by date.

I never liked the foursquare appeal of Paul's creation, especially its name. The ampersand was too banal for my taste, as was the lethargic reference to "text." I generally tried to overlook these matters, but every now and then they would get the better of me.

You seem to have made these views widely known right from the beginning of your involvement with the magazine.

Still, people were always complaining about something or other—the magazine was too short to stand out on newsstands, it was too hard to read, too theoretical, or too commercial, there wasn't enough art, and so on. Secretly, I tended to agree with them.

So you didn't take the criticism seriously?

It was hard to know what to do because the thrust of the criticism invariably centered on fantasy and Hallmark Channel questions to do with choice, as if everything had been the product of forethought and planning. Keeping things real never seemed to occur to anybody.

Playing down the role of choice in cultural work is a fairly meaningless gesture.

I wasn't so much referring to free choice as to the teleology of choice, the directive principle or final cause behind human endeavor. There weren't many real choices at stake in a non-profit exercise like *Art & Text*. That's why the appearance of my name on the imprint doesn't mean very much beyond my getting to witness it all firsthand.

You've opted out of seeing the magazine's history through the lens of influence or theory, but now you want us to believe that you were solely the victim of circumstance. Isn't it more about your fear of commitment?

Believe it or not, most of the time freedom of choice was not on the table, or somehow the choice was limited to doing nothing at all.

But you have to accept responsibility for everything that appeared in the magazine during your administration.

Yes, but that doesn't diminish the accidental factor. I don't want people thinking that what they see in the magazine represents my express point of view, or that I'm over the moon about the results. I still can't look at all of the issues without feeling a twinge of regret.

At the same time, the magazine's twenty-year run is a pretty outstanding achievement for such a single-minded venture.

The only choice that seems applicable in my case is standing by the magazine when no one else would. I suspect that restlessness of mind and operating outside the reach of institutions had more to do with what happened finally.

During the first half of the 1990s, the magazine started to develop content from Los Angeles. Susan Kandel contributed her first article, "Bad Girls Don't Cry," in September 1993 (No. 46), and she came on as contributing editor in September 1994 (No. 49). Can you talk about the origins of the L.A. connection?

The idea of moving operations to Los Angeles only emerged after six or so years of traveling there. I gradually began to make contact with people in the L.A. art world, including Amelia Jones and Susan Kandel. When I met Susan, she was an art critic at the *L.A. Times* and had recently terminated her association with a local art magazine called *Art.issues*. She seemed interested in helping to set up *Art & Text* as a viable alternative, so I said let's do it.

It can't have been so entirely spontaneous.

I can only put it down to a basic curiosity to see where her suggestion might lead. At first, it didn't extend much beyond setting up a distribution office on the West Coast and having greater access to writers there. I soon realized it was impossible for me to keep two offices going, so the plan rapidly shifted to L.A.

You could have kept the Sydney office going.

True, but I didn't think it would be necessary. Most things can be dealt with by email these days, and I was expecting a much larger potential market in the U.S. In the long run, the move was probably more due to weariness on my part with Australian cultural policy than a simple business decision.

Nonetheless, you had Susan and a number of Art Center interns to help you now.

Without wishing to sound ungrateful, none of that changed my impossible workload. Most people begin to faint dead away by three in the morning, when quite often I'm still up and working to meet a deadline. I don't understand what people expect. All I know is that no one ever seemed to hang around for very long.

Perhaps not everyone is as dedicated as you are.

I put it down to always wondering where all these bits of the puzzle might go and whether they could be shaped into an issue of an art magazine. Susan was terrifically dedicated, though. She even insisted on editing one issue from her hospital bed, after giving birth to her first daughter.

That doesn't sound like the situation you just described.

It's hard to explain. Susan was great, but she was never the editor in the way I had always been, which only exacerbated my frustration. Her input didn't extend much beyond securing writers, although she did try to put a human face on the discussion of art. That didn't prevent me from soon wearying of the columnists she tried to introduce in the magazine, because their avid self-promotion often seemed to overshadow whatever criticism they endorsed.

Does that mean she promoted work you didn't agree with?

I generally don't like to interfere in other people's work, but secretly think less of them if it fails to deliver. Intellectual life means everything to me, so I'm prone to forgive writers almost anything if their argument is well reasoned or daring. If it becomes evident this is not the case, I am capable of ignoring them.

Were the names that disappeared from the magazine's imprint also victims of your displeasure?

Nothing like that was ever usually necessary. It is common practice in the art world for people to lend their name to art magazines, but it often doesn't mean much beyond that. As for the more prominent names on the imprint, these were mostly short-term affairs with little, if any, direct involvement. There are a couple of notable exceptions, however.

Until the beginning of the 1990s, the magazine had comprised Australian, American, and European material. Did personal predisposition draw you to the U.S.?

I entertained the perhaps mistaken idea that the best art writers are mainly American, although now I'm not so sure.

Perhaps you are bound to find more good writers in a country of over 300 million people.

That's true. I was also thinking of the history of art criticism since Greenberg and, later, the *October* gang, etc. Now I am less secure in this belief.

You've often emphasized the superior editors in the U.S.

No doubt familiarity breeds contempt. When I edited Paul's collection of New York essays, I worked on the published versions and not, as he first wanted, the original texts, for the differences between them were as night and day. But one fact stood out from all the rest, which was that Paul's writing had improved immensely from his tutelage under the editors at *The New York Times*, *Vanity Fair*, and so on. Paul was a fairly inexperienced writer before he left Australia, but once he moved to New York and started doing laps of the press pool, he took off like a rocket. Nowadays, however, I suspect New York's authority is waning.

For a number of years, the magazine effectively straddled the Pacific with editorial input split between Los Angeles and Sydney. What problems or advantages did this create for the magazine?

It was just the same as before, but with a wider cast of players. I was really too frantic to think about much else.

Was your move to the U.S. reckless, considering much of the financial backing for the magazine was in Australia?

No question about it. But I couldn't have gone on receiving government support forever. I was already champing at the bit to leave.

What kind of reaction did you experience in Australia to your relocation to the U.S.?

A stunned silence, as if the magazine had never existed. Later, though, the grumbling began. Like I said, the whole point of Australian cultural life is to escape overseas, but if you succeed then everybody's nose gets out of joint. It's ridiculous. I truly hope this rash of national inadequacy is not permanent.

After more than twenty years of writing and publishing on art and ideas in Australia, did you leave with any sense of regret or concern for the energies you had invested there?

One always has regrets. The important thing is to forget about them.

You have written on the Australian condition and its long history. From whom else would one expect a direct answer to this question?

I was being direct.

After grappling with ideas of Australian distance and insularity, how could you quit the country without pause for reflection?

I think this is a question you're trying to ask yourself. As for me, my decision might seem like a mistake in hindsight. I just don't happen to see it that way. It was a perfectly reasonable thing to do under the circumstances, so I was prepared to see it through to the end.

Between 1999 and 2002, the last years of *Art & Text*, a new pool of U.S.-based writers brought a renewed energy to the magazine. You had already published Giovanni Intra, one of the more interesting writers and gallery owners then working in Los Angeles, when he still lived in New Zealand. But there were also many amazing contributions from writers like Sue Spaid, Terry R. Myers, Chris Kraus, Peter Lunenfeld, Laurence A. Rickels, Frances Stark, Nancy Princenthal, and David Hunt. In collaboration with these writers, you seemed to present a particularly upbeat slant on the local scene.

It was too upbeat, if you ask me. Much of the selection you describe reflects Susan's take on the larger aspirations of the L.A. scene. My input into content and certain long-term interests prevailed, however, as can be seen from the special "Nord Art" issue (No. 66, August–October 1999) I put together after a studio tour of Scandinavian countries. But the strain was beginning to show. When I offered Susan an experimental text on the question of methamphetamine use in the art world, called "No Punding Zone" (No. 74, August–October 2001), she conceded—pointedly perhaps—that it probably wouldn't be wise to list it on the contents page, suggesting it be left as an unspecified "surprise." As I didn't immediately know how to take her response, I went along with it. But this compromise sheds much light on my growing discomfort with the way things stood.

But these are such fantastic issues that it's hard to believe what you're saying.

It's interesting to hear your description of them, because for me a shadow began to loom over the entire L.A. operation.

There must have been other factors at the time to make you feel that way.

Certainly the reality of becoming a creature of the establishment soon began to hit home, complicated by my general reluctance to abandon the course of action I had entered into.

What do you mean by "creature of the establishment"?

I don't happen to welcome a high degree of social visibility, which is what heading up an international art magazine requires. My dilemma was that I could never find anyone willing or capable enough to play this role, so I was always stuck with it. Eventually, I decided I wouldn't do it anymore.

So the problem didn't have so much to do with the material the magazine was publishing.

There was nothing especially wrong with what Susan was doing. But at the same time, I didn't see much evidence that it was succeeding critically or commercially, either. In many ways the situation was worse than before, when at least I was only accountable to myself.

What about the new design by Denise Gonzales Crisp, then head of the design unit at Art Center?

Denise wanted to apply her own theories to the magazine, theories which principally involved mixing up fonts and treating text as a design element—"all wrong," she once admitted to me, in the established order of design. Soon a couple of galleries complained that the text was illegible, the art was being used to make a point, there was no way to tell where the articles began or ended, etc. None of that was exactly untrue, yet it was also a blunt indictment of the basic conservatism of the L.A. art world. It was only my refusal to bend to these lame protests that prevented me from confronting the matter sooner.

You didn't like her design?

I didn't dislike it, but then I love to experiment. In the end, we parted ways. Susan soon followed, on the advice—so she said—of her accountant. I suppose I'd made it clear to both of them that the present arrangement was rapidly becoming unworkable, which was not at all what I had intended to happen. So I continued the magazine on my own, aided and abetted by Micah Heimlich, a young architect from Texas. Together, we designed those last three issues (Nos. 76–78). You have to remember that in the past I played an active role in the design process. Now thanks to Micah's unique computer skills, I could begin to take the magazine in the direction to which I always aspired.

You've often spoken about the magazine as a burden you wanted to pass on to someone else. Did the departure of Susan Kandel and Denise Gonzales Crisp force you to reconsider the viability of the magazine?

If the magazine was a burden to me, then it must have been one I perversely welcomed somehow. I certainly realized that all this devotion curtailed other ambitions I might have had, but at the same time I can't say these tradeoffs wouldn't have occurred anyway. I happen to like publishing magazines as much as I dislike it. Call it insane or even self-indulgent, but at least I've tried to disclose traces of my frustration as I moved along.

Giovanni Intra died the same year the magazine ended. He was an important contributor to those final issues. Was this a traumatic event for you and the magazine?

I never really saw much of Giovanni after I moved to L.A., so I don't know anything about his personal life. Most of the time he was very busy, first as a student at

Art Center, then establishing a gallery in Chinatown with some of his student friends, and finally traveling overseas. He did try to get me to go to dinner at his apartment a few times, but I always seemed to wriggle out of it. I spoke to him briefly a short time before his death in New York, when he mentioned some trouble to do with a girlfriend.

But you knew him going way back, didn't you?

Giovanni was a genuinely nice guy who seemed in his element in the L.A. art world. Now I think no one knew him at all. He was a brilliant personality and a natural at running a gallery, however. His loss was keenly felt. I witnessed his charms firsthand at a dinner party held by L.A. gallery owner Marc Selwyn—for Elizabeth Peyton, I believe. Mink Stole also attended, as did Shaun Caley (the director of Regen Projects), and a few other notables. Giovanni acquitted himself superbly at that dubious affair, I thought.

Did Giovanni know you were ill?

He was one of the few people I told. Not long after that, he died of a drug overdose in New York. It was then that I realized I'd lost one of the few people worth knowing in Los Angeles.

His essay on Berlin artist Isa Genzken was to be included in the final issue of _Art & Text_, which was never published.

Correct. Before closing down the magazine, I handed Giovanni's text to Greg Burke at the Govett-Brewster Art Gallery in New Zealand, who published it.

What did you go through during this difficult period?

Don't forget the 2000 election hijack and 9/11, both catastrophic shocks to the American world system. I suppose we all try to make do during tough times, as there isn't any point to giving up or giving in. But I consider myself lucky to have been around during these historic times, notwithstanding the personal and collective cost.

Closing down the magazine after many years of all-consuming activity must have been a disappointment to you.

I never conceived of it in these black or white terms, but as an unavoidable hiatus in activity. And that is exactly what happened. After all, I have a bigger fight on my hands.

You've said you never necessarily thought of *Art & Text* as an art magazine.

I prefer to think about my publications as a prolonged series of thought experiments in critical writing. I have often asked myself what happens when publishing is no longer about knowledge or power. Even though that is a role it is almost doomed to play, I have never allowed myself to believe it is its only role.

After the last issue of *Art & Text*, you took off for a year or so before embarking on *artUS*—the first issue appeared in November 2003. This new magazine emerged in a completely different context from the one that spawned *Art & Text*. Do you, though, see it as part of the same story?

I had the idea for this new magazine long ago, back in Australia. I thought of locating it in a number of different countries, with a central office coordinating everything online. The magazine is essentially devoted to short and extended reviews, with a few inserted features, but the boundary lines are never clearly drawn. For me, the art review is an important literary genre, unique to the art world. It may even be the *genius loci* of all critical language. Art magazines are generally conservative in their design and content, and in most instances indistinguishable from the press at large. I wanted to carve a different kind of object out of the same material.

If the end of *Art & Text* was a hiatus before a new beginning, but its successor belongs to a completely different story, where is the continuity? Don't both publications belong to the same trajectory of activism, one that spans your entire career in publishing and editing?

There is no continuity at all, just a series of Benjaminian emergency stops. My fascination with publishing over the years has had little to do with high theory or the art world as such, nor was I concerned with expressing some political or sexual point of view. At this late date, it all seems to distract from the principal purpose, which was to further my research in critical writing. This is why I put up with all the fuss and bother, the frayed nerves and temperamental personalities, the avarice and class betrayals. It's not up to me to say whether it was finally worth it. I do know that the magazine helped a lot of people get to where they are today. I hope they understand better a little of what made it possible.

Rob McKenzie wishes to acknowledge Roslyn Oxley, Ross Harley, Jeff Gibson, and Vivienne Shark LeWitt for their invaluable assistance in preparing for this online interview, which took place between April 22 and October 19, 2007.

3. Peripheral Burnout

Paul Foss in correspondence with Rex Butler

REX BUTLER: **Paul, you wrote what I consider to be the definitive Australian art essay of the 1980s, "Theatrum Nondum Cognitorum." It had an enormous impact on me when I read it as a first-year university student, and it was undoubtedly the inspiration behind Paul Taylor's** *Popism* **exhibition.**[1] **Can you tell me a little about the story behind it? What were you reading then? Why would someone of your intellectual background be drawn to writing an essay about (the impossibility of) Australian identity?**

PAUL FOSS: It is interesting you see a connection between "Theatrum" and *Popism*. That possibility never occurred to me, but Paul was a shrewd observer of art world trends. For instance, those two Baudrillard translations he had me do for his *Post-Pop Art* monograph[2] were a deliberate attempt to bring about an alliance between the East Village crowd and Washington Square, between second-generation Warholism and the theoretical work of Columbia and New York Universities. A similar alliance may have occurred in the Melbourne context with *Popism*, but I never saw this show or knew anything about it.

As for "Theatrum," collecting back-to-front or feet-to-feet references is a continuing hobby of mine. I suppose this makes me a prototypical Antipodean. On the other hand, you could say the essay is the *summa confessorum* of my troubled affair with Australian manners. It appeared toward the end of 1980, at the culmination of publishing various underground magazines and books on new critical theory in Sydney. But as it happened to straddle a transitional moment in my life, when I more or less abandoned academic life, the text must still retain traces of self-questioning and doubt. It's easy to imagine this uncertainty being transferred to the semiotics theme of the Sydney University conference where it was first delivered, reemerging as the mapping of identity at large.

Not incidentally, as a child I was forever drawing maps of imaginary islands. As with most people, for me islands conjure up dreams of paradise, as well as desertion, isolation, inundation. This fascination also fueled many travels to the Pacific islands. A close friend and I were once almost drowned during a violent storm out at sea near a remote corner of the Solomon Islands. We ended up running aground on a submerged reef, but our Melanesian guides somehow managed to get us back into the canoe while towering waves crashed all around. The coral just below the surface cut our feet to ribbons. In my mind, that near miss will always be associated with the brooding menace of islands.

It perplexes me why people tend to see this essay through the looking glass of postmodernism, when in fact it is a fairly ordinary "summit" exposition of contradictory views in the classic *sic et non* tradition. My conceit, if you like, was to put the country's core myth—the supreme antiquity and contrariness of the world's youngest, least understood, and smallest continent—under the microscope, pitting the known against the unknown like cartographers of old. The pull or traction of this Platonic fable of polar opposites has left its mark on every aspect of Australian life. If you ask me, the mapping of Terra Australis Incognita and the search for Atlantis are mythically inseparable.

One of the theoretical influences behind "Theatrum" was undoubtedly Jean Baudrillard. You've had a vexed relationship with Baudrillard over the years. Later, for instance, in the André Frankovits-edited volume *Seduced and Abandoned: The Baudrillard Scene*,[3] timed to appear before Baudrillard's first Australian visit (at the *Futur*Fall* conference in Sydney in 1984), you publicly rejected Baudrillard.

Seduced and Abandoned was mostly the creation of Meaghan Morris, who for some time had gone about town loudly denouncing Baudrillard's hyperbolic "the end of the real" as implicitly endorsing the status quo—as one said back then. Yet, to Meaghan's credit, her target was only ever the hype and not the philosopher himself. Privately, Meaghan told me she admired many of Baudrillard's ideas.

Whatever one might think of this act of pamphleteering today, it did help to stir things up at a pivotal moment in the Sydney underground. By around 1984, a clan mentality had started to set in once various factions began to capitalize on what later became postmodernism, taking it as gospel that a critical theory is made from whole cloth rather than being the medium, to quote Walter Benjamin, in which ancient injustices lie buried, ready to be exhumed and entered into evidence. Baudrillard was not the only figure to suffer this fate, however much he may have even encouraged it.

"Despero Ergo Sum," the essay I contributed to Meaghan's book, should be seen in the light of these comments. It sought to reintroduce nihilism as an inherent threat to certain types of political posturing, mostly those fanning the embers of a pretend collectivity, whether old guard or part of the now. But the bets were hedged both ways. The new theoretical materialism that arose after the countercultural bubble burst had set in motion what we see today, replacing hard-line institutions with new, "stickier" ones. I simply pointed to the haunted scene or lineage of this radical breakthrough. Sometimes just repeating an old boo word is enough to send people scurrying.

To carry on from the last question, it's notable that in some of your "gay" writings—say, the little book on Juan Davila, *The Mutilated Pieta* (1985)—you look for sources of cultural resistance in places that Baudrillard would not and are also resigned or pessimistic at moments when Baudrillard wouldn't be.

All of my writings are queer, surely. Just like G.K. Chesterton in his 1905 collection of short stories, *The Club of Queer Trades*, political simulacra and counterespionage intrigue me, the only difference between us being the kind of subterfuge involved. Sometimes, as happened with my text accompanying Davila's 1985 painting *Holy Family*, the immediate goal concerns censorship and disappearance—in this case, the persistent seizure of the artist's sexually charged work. Or I might attempt to simulate the very argument against which the opposite opinion is pitted, only to draw out some of its hidden assumptions, as occurs in "Despero Ergo Sum." The Cartesian pun is a clue to this little deception.

I don't understand why this ruse of mine—which, after all, is a reasonably familiar one in the history of the novel and other types of satirical literature—might be thought resigned or pessimistic. I suppose it all depends on whether drawing close to the abyss of appearances is a liberating or frightening experience for people, even if escaping its fatal attraction seems impossible. To counter the falling sensation caused by this introduction to the treacherous slope of reason, *The Mutilated Pieta* proposed an *orphan* subjectivity as a way of accommodating what I termed "[living] on the edge of an infinitesimal line that leads nowhere and figures nothing"— referring, of course, to the mythic Antipodean condition. Philosophers often describe the comparison of dissimilar terms as a type of class reductionism, but here I was using the word only in the scientific sense of an orphan tsunami, meaning a destructive event that is not local in origin but caused by very distant forces. An *orphan subjectivity*, then, would be one experienced at a distance, making the local environment of perceptions and behaviors unstable, as must surely happen when the earth's magnetic poles reverse. I can't speak for others, but to me this seems no more depressing than the inevitability of an asteroid strike.

It is interesting, given you were one of the inspirations behind Taylor's *Popism*, that you were suspicious of the logic of appropriation. I remember an interview you did with Imants Tillers, "Mammon or Millennial Eden?" in *Art & Text* (Nos. 23/24, March–May 1987), where you worry that the act of artistic appropriation simply leaves the quoted text or object where it was before.

That discussion with Imants was my first published art interview, so I suspect a lot of it was just playing tag. But whatever I was trying to say about appropriation, which has always intrigued me, the concept certainly resists easy formulation. Looking back through art history since earliest times, what stands out is appropriation's essentially spectral character, those ghostly effects kith and kin to all feats of reproduction. Appropriation, as I understand it, is technically a form of haunting, in the sense of trying to inhabit something without a proper habitat or sanction. You only need look at the behind-the-scenes machinations of the art world to understand why this phantom continues to galvanize it. In the broader context of postmodernism, however, appropriation is probably not a new strategy and may even be a cover for the continuation of modernism by other means.

It also intrigued me, insofar as "Theatrum" was a text so far ahead of its time, that soon after publishing it you more or less gave up writing. You turned to editing and writing pieces in a variety of authorial voices, or even pseudonymously. What were the limits of academic writing as they appeared to you then?

Toward the end of the 1980s, I no longer belonged to either the academic or radical camps. I wanted to continue writing, but wasn't entirely sure if doing the magazine gave me the time to pursue this interest adequately. So I increasingly turned my attention to using editing or formal contextualization as a sort of writing, molding a found series of editable materials into a fragmentary opus in its own right.

There are many precedents for this kind of experiment, among them the sampling of random images, texts, and commercial signs in Benjamin's 1930s *Archive*. Yet even if it could be argued that behind this experiment lies the desire for anonymity, there is still no reason to assume that this refers to anything more than the habits and transferences of the act of archiving itself, as undoubtedly it was for Benjamin. But it is also a commonsense response to the daily toil as editor, freeing me to instill what is generally a thankless task with supplementary relevance.

Many of my editorial hauntings have been unavoidable consequences of this archival drudgery. It explains why I have used different names to signal what is already being said elsewhere under the guise of no less authentic voices, which seems to me a perfect corollary of the writing experiment I just described. The same argument applies to a number of texts where I present as my own independent creation a revised and completely rewritten version of a thematically related essay by someone else. This isn't so much about plagiarism or pulling strings behind the scenes, although I accept the impulse to do so always exists, but more about showcasing the constructed nature of all published writings. As happens when actors suddenly interrupt a play to talk directly to the audience, these plot derailments help to shatter the spectacle of writing.

You later became editor of *Art & Text*. First of all, I know you had a very hardheaded attitude toward writing and publishing. You wanted the magazine and the writing in it to be slick and professional. Sometimes your turning away from the usual laissez-faire attitude of small art journals was so extreme as to be almost parodic. In general, what kinds of attitudes did you want to bring into the world of Australian art publishing as it was then?

The aura of publishing is indeed a pox on everyone concerned. Although I didn't set out to follow in the footsteps of most art magazines, where unbridled ambition is often confused with criticism, I have needed to find my own way around this dilemma. Apart from trying to inject a little order and uniformity into the published material, I never believed any of that went as far as it could have gone or demanded. I simply experimented with the experiments of others. In other words, I allowed writers to argue whatever they wanted, but only so long as the rules of the game they themselves had put in place were carried through to the letter. Raw sentiment, for instance, is often removed as a distraction from the demands of critical reasoning. For me, it comes down to a question of concentration. I have always tried to excavate the actual thought processes and arguments of writers rather than impose the niceties of language on them from on high.

In the case of *Art & Text*, my principal concern was to position the art and writing in something like a rotating gallery, rather than enter into the fake appearances of art culture itself, in which image and text seem doomed to play a secondary role. I have always admired and tried to safeguard the unique conceptual framework of art discourses, which are perhaps a little looser than most other critical genres. But there are inherent dangers in this laxity, which often endorses spur-of-the-moment formulations as somehow artistic and therefore authentic. True, I haven't actively encouraged this approach, but neither is it impossible to find plenty of instances to the contrary in what I have published over the years.

Paul Taylor, in his final projects, such as *After Andy: SoHo in the Eighties* (1995), wanted to write a secret history of contemporary art to make clear the unspoken influence of dealers, art advisers, and clients. In a sense, he wanted to take the power of taste making away from the critics and curators, and even the artists, and hand it over to those with money. How sympathetic are you to this attitude? Do you believe—of course, it was self-contradictory in Taylor's case, who was a critic himself—in the impotence of art criticism?

Irrespective of what I believe, it would be useless to protest. Nor would simply affirming the contrary change real stakes in the art world. Even trying to rethink the polar opposites of this debate outside the toolbox is tantamount to a kind of withdrawal, as is signaling the emergence of an advanced, as yet non-contradictory form of criticism. But whatever has happened to critical language in the meantime, we're still too close to it to know whether its value has fallen or, to use Klossowski's term, it has become *priceless*. Art writing today is worth no more and often considerably less than the price of a full-page ad in the mainstream press. None of this is new or even newsworthy. For ours is increasingly an age of augmented ears and not eyes, so even pronouncing on the impotence of art criticism is something that can only be put about or bought into, not literally seen or read on the page— without mentioning blogging, twittering, and all the other reverberations of the art world gramophone. As for Paul, I'm not sure he wanted to hand over taste to Wall Street in the way you suggest. Even if he had, arguing that art has now sold out is hardly earth-shattering.

When you finally became sole editor of *Art & Text*, your aesthetic—and it continues in *artUS*—was different from Taylor's. It is too simple to call it camp or even queer, even though you ran notable features on Pierre et Gilles and Gilbert & George and did that special issue called "The 'Thing' " (No. 20, February–April 1986). But you do seem to have a kind of taste for the far-out and aesthetically extravagant, from Hany Armanious and Mikala Dwyer in Australia to Jessica Stockholder and Jason Rhoades internationally. It's not a straightforward anti-aesthetic. On the contrary, it's a deliberately avant-garde form of aesthetics. Do you have in mind a particular look to the art you feature?

It's a mistake to assume that what I have shown in the magazine somehow represents my own taste. That, in my opinion, would be a misuse of one's position as publisher, which is something I take very seriously, especially as I've seen a lot of evidence to the contrary elsewhere over the years. The whole point of a critical art magazine is to solicit discussion around the ideas suggested by the art, not to further the visual or market appreciation of art, which is an entirely different exercise and well served by the commercial literature. I certainly don't dislike visual art, as some have claimed, although I do think this is the unstated bias of a lot of exponents of cultural analysis. Nor would I go so far as to claim for the magazine a rigid avant-garde perspective, which goes against everything I have ever believed. If anything, my views on art have generally erred on the side of caution, because I believe it usually requires a fair amount of time and reflection for the clouds to part so the material arguments of the zeitgeist can come through. Spectacle, which is both the constant whip and guiding spirit of art criticism, is the very foundation the magazine tried to establish itself *against*, hollowing it out from underneath as it were.

By and large, people don't really understand the role publishers or editors play. Gilbert & George's asshole—which Paul suggested, by the way—may seem like a deliberately queer gesture, but I never thought about it in that fashion. To my mind, it had more to do with the various Lacanian philosophies espoused in that issue. When choosing material, I generally consider a number of factors, such as readability on the page, photographic quality, degree of exposure, found associations between images, and things like currency, but maneuvering at the edge of the new isn't the same as blindly giving way to it. There isn't much here in the way of individual taste, only professional courtesy and the slow, patient unraveling of critical exchange. Most of the time, I only put a certain artwork on the cover to test its assigned shelf life, which is not an aesthetic act in my view but something much more synoptic.

What hopes do you ultimately invest in the kind of criticism of the visual arts that you have spent so much of your life fostering and enabling? You have become increasingly interested in classical music of late. Is this because whatever ambitions you once had for the visual arts and the writing about it have not been realized? Might we even compare you to someone like Adorno, both in the aspirations you once had to a resistant art and the melancholy you now feel with the apparent victory of the *culture industry*?

At the limit, even despondency has its uses. Don't forget that melancholy not only evokes sadness and despair, but can also act as a kind of testing ground for aesthetic imagination. Adorno's idea of regressive listening certainly leads to very interesting critical possibilities in the visual arts, as one already sees in the various forms of sound art. Still, you don't need Adorno to prove a systematic correlation between synesthesia in the arts or the cross-activation of visual and acoustic neurons in the media cortex. Today's music and fine art differ only in their degree of sensory overload, but that is already a very provocative idea. My views on art, however, are not directly related to objective, or political, resistance, but to its very opposite, something like terminal burnout or instructive melancholy. As Shakespeare so correctly observes in *Sonnet 64*, "Ruin hath taught me thus to ruminate." It is cultural resistance that has always intrigued me, the aesthetic or literary resistance to ruin and rumination, and the way that resistance can reveal all sorts of regressive tendencies. It is not about what I think is crucial or critically valid, but about finding common cause for rumination in the lapses and lacunae of contemporary thought. I may not have succeeded in making my publishing strategy always clear, but the extant record is ripe for analysis.

This interview represents responses, written between October 8, 2007, and January 19, 2008, to a set questionnaire supplied by Rex Butler.

1.   Melbourne: National Gallery of Victoria, 1982.
2.   Cambridge, Mass.: MIT Press, 1989.
3.   Sydney: Stonemoss, 1984.

4. Woes of the Pharisees

Paul Foss interviewed by Simon Rees

SIMON REES: Why did the magazine's name and format keep changing over the years?

PAUL FOSS: It's no great surprise I never liked the name. I even said as much to Paul Taylor. The double handle is too schooled for my liking, and the ampersand caused all sorts of trouble for design and publicity. Paul was too proud a parent to bother with such petty details. At least *October*, which was the main precursor of *Art & Text*, exhibited some panache and historical irony in its choice of name.

At first I was consoled by the thought I would soon be jumping ship. The signs were hardly auspicious. A year or so earlier, Paul (and his lawyer brother Greg) had sued a Sydney-based publication, *Art & a Texta*—the latter is a local brand of permanent marker—for satirizing the magazine's name. The libel suit was written up in all the Australian newspapers, to great hilarity of course, and in clear detriment to the best interests of contemporary art. Paul found it hugely amusing. Many didn't agree. But the action he took was also rather shrewd because it succeeded in bringing national attention to the fledgling magazine. What Paul failed to grasp is that it only aggravated pre-existing criticism of the magazine's alleged elitism and nonconformity. Paradoxically, the lawsuit only corroborated the legitimacy of the libel.

In my mind, the magazine's name became synonymous with the general mess I inherited when Paul left for New York. This feeling finally shifted to the ampersand itself, to which I ended up becoming highly allergic. I always wondered what this lexical leftover from eighteenth-century novels and broadsheets—so out of place today, unless you happen to be an indie band—had to do with the concept of a contemporary art magazine. Was it a sort of John Nixon cross, I wondered? However, Paul's masthead at least had the advantage of implying a level playing field for art and art writing, somewhat in the mold of Lawrence Weiner's conceptual text pieces. Anyway, that was in the 1980s. Soon enough the title began to sound dated. It failed to compute or stick in people's minds, or such was my experience, even long after the magazine's imagined success. As time went by, I grew ever more weary of having to repeat the name.

Aficionados of the magazine will note the many strategies I deployed over the years for playing down or erasing the damned ampersand. First, I replaced it with a plus sign, then a forward slash, and then, by total elimination, contracted the title into a single word (requiring dropping a *T*). I can't say any of this had the desired effect. It probably made the situation worse, as proof positive of an ongoing identity crisis.

All of this would easily lend itself to semiotic or deconstructive analysis, certainly when entertaining the notion of serial publishing as a kind of *Bildungsroman* or novel of character formation. I'm obviously too biased to carry out the task myself—psychologists call this the "actor-observer bias." It's difficult for me not to fall prey to the romantic idea of publishers wandering nomadically through the narrow passes and dark forests of collected wisdom, encountering fresh challenges at every turn. Yet I can still recognize the dangers. This must be why, just as Hansel and

Gretel left a trail of breadcrumbs to mark their way, I too like to plan an escape route in advance.

You are also correct in assuming many of these refinements were related to changes in the size and format of the magazine, most of which occurred for obvious reasons. This is typical behavior for all serial workers, whether they are magazine publishers or stage actors. Leaving aside questions of interpretation or performance, the sheer boredom of constantly having to play the same part leads to metaphrasis and contextual sleight of hand, if only to remain sane. It's all part of the same journey of identity, of the same retracing of steps.

When Paul died in 1992, I wanted to resolve the matter once and for all by changing the magazine's name to "Taylor's," which I thought both fitting and commercially viable, but everybody I knew threw a fit when I mentioned it to them.

Did publishing a lot of commercial gallery advertising affect the editorial content?

It's not that Paul Taylor's early issues didn't have a lot of advertising as well. Naturally, he expected me to keep the level going after his departure, but I am not very good at that sort of thing—the soliciting, social side of advertising, not so much its actual design or strategizing. The thorn festered in my side for a number of years, until around *Art & Text* 36 (May 1990), when it more or less fell into other hands. I was always content to put my time and effort into the material published in the magazine, hoping it would sell itself.

This doesn't mean I was ever comfortable with raising the advertising bar in *Art & Text*. I like the visual impact of different kinds of image spreads, but it's often more trouble than it's worth. Juggling a lot of advertising is simply asking for trouble in the editorial department, without mentioning the accounting department. Yet I don't have anything against the culture of advertising, whose tricks of the trade clearly resemble those of the art world. What I like to remind people about art advertising is how it conceals its real message, which is that branding or framing art is more desirable than the act of creating it.

It's hard not to be a hypocrite when it comes to the art world. It is easy to get on your high horse over insider trading, nepotism, disinformation, and the like. But why should the art world be expected to behave any differently from the world at large? Is the art world part of the empirical, work-a-day world, or not? My approach has simply been to accept the inevitability of the art world and try to work with it, if only to draw this inevitability into the open. It's fine by me if artists are reviewed alongside advertisements from their galleries, so long as the most scrupulous standards are applied to their work—even though the editor responsible may need nerves of steel to see the operation through. I believe this bias to be essential for preserving the critical spirit in publishing, not by refusing to follow party lines, but by testing the utmost lengths to which the discussion will go to save the appearances.

Does *artUS*'s jettisoning of extensive advertising represent a critical reaction to commercial pressures?

I don't know what you are referring to other than the fact *artUS* is a more experimental entity. As I said before, I like the opportunities advertising affords for revealing how the art world essentially works. But when all is said and done, that doesn't change the system very much. What matters more to me is the genuine article, not its appearance or branding identity. Despite various comments I have made to the contrary, I secretly enjoy the art world and try to support it as best I can. At the same time, the very nature of art publishing has changed. Online options have largely expanded the publisher's brief today.

On the whole, I don't indulge in the sort of reactive criticism you suggest. Resisting the economic motive behind art commerce makes less sense to me than realizing that this motive is only part of a much larger cultural mechanism for circulating the ideas and images of art. Most advertising is entirely self-serving, yet that doesn't necessarily limit its corresponding—or accidental—value as critique, even as art. Nor is this without interest when strategizing design or editorial content. Advertising only points to the reality of which so much of it seems incapable of disabusing itself, making it inimical to the truth effect of publishing.

What is the main difference for you between publishing in the U.S. and publishing in Australia (and, for that matter, from Los Angeles rather than New York or Boston)?

There is none, really, but I imagine that is due to rapid acclimatization. Individuals obviously vary from place to place, as do specific cultural and business practices. Even so, publishing can take place almost anywhere today given the right equipment and broadband access. Thus armed, the accidental publisher is ideally situated to track the virtual everywhere (and nowhere) of global simultaneity. I'm not saying that the now almost universal proximity of the very near and the very far works the same way for everyone, but it has certainly informed my practice.

Besides, I imagine what you're getting at—especially since in the West the practical differences are minimal anyway—is not an external change of address but the internal exile one experiences upon leaving one country for another. I have tended to ignore this, arguing that Australians already exist in a state of permanent exile—from their past and future, their interior and exterior, their subjective and objective life. This is ultimately why I find the distinction between inhabiting different countries to be minimal, because internal exile is something you carry about with you wherever you are. The real question, rather, is what happens when you realize there is nowhere else to go.

How competitive have you found international art publishing to be?

All human affairs are competitive, so why single out publishing? The main issue for me concerns the presumed higher calling of art, even though it bears every similarity to the vocation of the world at large and may even be its consummation, because it simultaneously disavows or conceals it. What makes the art world so unique is that it demands to be treated as *both* special and commonplace, as above reproach yet also secretly admired for playing by the rules. I wouldn't go so far as to call this wrong or hypocritical, but it is revealing to see the art world for what it is and not what it pretends to be.

On the other hand, competition is a practical way for social institutions to set boundaries for themselves or settle disagreements. Envious artists sometimes sabotage their peers by refusing to exhibit alongside them, forcing them out of plum galleries. High-end art magazines regularly demand loyalty from their reviewers, partly to keep them for themselves and partly to secure advertising territory. Important galleries will ban publications if their reportage doesn't fit the standard line, cutting the umbilical cord of supply and demand. All this is to be expected, and it would be rather idealistic if it weren't. My response is generally to ignore the competition, mainly for fear of being dragged into it.

What other art magazines, including titles that may have folded, do you admire?

Early on I kept up with the majors, but soon fell out of the habit. Call it a professional hazard if you will, but I don't happen to find knowing what the rest are doing to be particularly helpful. Nor do I take pleasure in magazines as many people thankfully do. Most art rags seem to me like wasted opportunities, being mainly about product placement, while their covers are often inexplicably conservative, certainly compared to architecture and design magazines. I used to think this stuffiness was a refusal to take up the challenge of art, but now see it as a deliberate and even perceptive course of action. The reason may be that many galleries look down their noses at any attempt to digress from the founding myths of the art they show, as if encouraging it to break free of this lineage is an affront to decorum. I have tried to draw attention to this closely guarded reserve of art magazines, but it is perilous to ignore it completely. In many respects, the pursuit of art criticism is only permissible at the discretion of existing institutions. This is one obstacle to producing an art magazine, but it also provides plenty of opportunities to blow the lid on it.

In your opinion, what are the critical stakes in art publishing today?

Now that the art world is a fully inducted member of the society of the spectacle, there hardly seems any point to gratuitous discussion at the expense of sales. The discussion, such as it is, is geared either toward those who aspire to enter the profession of art writing, or to feed the machinery of insider trading. But as for art criticism as such, it is rare, especially in art magazines. Again, none of this would be worth mentioning were it not for the pretense of it being otherwise.

In contrast, profound technological change has altered the stakes of art publishing. What was once a cumbersome and rarefied process of isolated professions and techniques has now been replaced by instantaneous global access to information. Likewise, the object of publishing has atomized and disappeared into an infinite network of interactive feedback (blogs, YouTube, etc.). Given the escalating costs of geographical distribution, the time will come when the bulk of the information product will be purchased online—not so much read as scanned, downloaded, absorbed (like moisturizer). Thanks to the example of Google and other search engines, advertising is now dragged along in the process. This does not mean that hard copy will entirely disappear, only that henceforth it will be the cover for online trading.

It is of course useless to resist the new technologies and their repercussion. Increasingly, those who hold the technological stakes will also hold the critical ones, and that is a fact we need to face up to now. It's not difficult to see where all this is heading as most of the groundwork is already in place. As we see happening in CNN polling and call-in voting on *American Idol*, the real task of instantaneous electronic information is to preserve the appearance of an autonomous network of consumers, rather than to offer actual soundings of genuine opinions or behaviors, which become identical to whatever interpretation gets thrown at them. What sticks today is mainly the result of this all-embracing photonic dimension. Art magazines may be a bit slow to embrace the new interactive system, but they too can't stop moving in that direction.

In recent years, *Third Text* has been sold to Routledge and *New Left Review* to Verso to guarantee each magazine's survival. Have you explored any such option for *artUS* or the *Art & Text* back catalogue?

One can just as easily say this is equivalent to the death of these publications. Leaving aside the obvious objections, they can no longer be in remission what they once were in poor health. Survival is not necessarily the best outcome in professional life, since ultimate disappearance may be preferable to living forever in the shadow of eternity.

***Frieze* magazine has evolved into an art fair and *Artforum* into *artforum.com*. Do you think the digitalization of culture and the expansion of the physical infrastructure of art, combined with easy access to plane travel, make publishing redundant? Or will digitalization be the savior of magazine back catalogues?**

Again, the digitalization of the art press is both our savior and our cross to bear. The transformations you describe regarding these two publications may represent a satisfactory outcome at the purely monetary level, but it also speaks volumes about their sliding fortunes in the value of art criticism. This begs the question of what art magazines precisely sell today other than their complicity in the art of selling. Art criticism now seems like a former mistress whose sudden appearance at the wedding banquet is a huge embarrassment.

I am interested in digitalization's positive impact on design and production. My publishing career extends from the old cut-and-paste days through primitive computers and beyond, so the difference between what I can do now and what I could do then is truly amazing. Given the right technical assistance, it's possible to treat the magazine page as a canvas, layering it with intricate nuances and brushstrokes to carve out found associations between words and images. The advertising industry is a wizard at this kind of digital magic, and its example is truly contagious, making it increasingly difficult to tell where ads and articles begin and end in most glossies. It's a shame the same can't be said for many of the world's fine-art publications, which seem stuck in some McCarthyite era where everything is stitched up, drawn and quartered.

You implicitly raise an important point about the future of publishing. If you ask me, trade magazines and online sampling are not exactly forms of publishing—the term means to make public what was previously concealed or poorly recognized. Publishing, in fact, requires a society of independent readers. Our virtual society is not as concerned with global readership as it pretends, but rather with the spectacularization of all reading, its reduction to a basic reflex of familiar brands or identities. Regardless of whether hard copy survives, digitalization might spell the end of publishing after all.

You have often said, "curators can't write." Is this a practical response to all the overworked and administratively focused curators we have seen emerge since the 1990s, or is it an observation of a deeper tension between curating as a materialist discipline and writing as an idealist, research-based pursuit?

It's not so much a fact as a provocation. I used to say it to shock people into thinking about the art world chain of command. Nor is it so surprising, given the curator's job description. But I've never been exactly sure what curators do. In Europe, they are sometimes sensibly called art historians. My provocation, however, applies just as much to the people who do magazines, who increasingly look and behave like Eddy and Patsy in *Absolutely Fabulous*. I have often wondered if the failure to organize thoughts on paper, or the reluctance of everyone concerned to admit this to themselves, is the main reason why people end up in curatorial and publishing jobs. If true, it would speak volumes about the demise of critical writing in the art world.

Over the years, many people have accused you of running the magazine with a queer agenda or bias, to the exclusion of other positions or interests, as if magazines are supposed to be all-inclusive. To me, any such bias seemed a natural corollary to the strength of artists like Félix González-Torres and the young Juan Davila; the writings of Foucault, Deleuze, Guattari, and Craig Owens; the figure of André Gide as a champion of literary experimentation, discovery, translation, criticism, and editing (which I can see in the magazine and in your own work); and the urgency of the HIV/AIDS crisis from the late 1980s onwards. I'd like to hear an answer to those critics and this accusation.

As Charlie Chaplin once said to Einstein, "The people applaud me because everyone understands me, and they applaud you because no one understands you." I wonder if this idea might work in the reverse, meaning that people precisely applaud what they don't understand only in order to decry what they do understand. This is perhaps why I don't have long-term intellectual or political affairs, just a series of one-night stands. It is true that I was once heavily involved in gay liberation, but that was long before I started doing *Art & Text*. What we are basically left with is a series of hollow projections that occurred for no other reason than to provide a convenient alibi for attacking the unaligned critical positions of the magazine. Homosexuals have always made ideal scapegoats.

Moreover, the charge you describe is not borne out by the facts. The gay material in the 8,000-or-so pages of *Art & Text* is overall miniscule. To me, it is somewhat like Janet Jackson's infamous "wardrobe malfunction"—the momentary flash was blown all out of proportion only to safeguard the appearance of normal programming. The same idea applies to the magazine's allegedly naughty covers, principally Nos. 20, 48, 62, and 66 (notwithstanding the topless Kylie Minogue on the cover of No. 60). Whatever the reasons for featuring the images in question, most of which were surprisingly banal, those complaints prove just how difficult it remains to depart from normal programming in the art world.

The art world often seems to operate as a moral majority in relation to many alternative pursuits or practices, probably in denial of its own interests. Could you speak about this bigotry in terms of your own experience?

Psychologists call this tendency to blame others for your own faults the "fundamental attribution error," meaning that people tend to overstress the importance of dispositional or personality-based explanations for behaviors while playing down contextual explanations. When we observe others, the person concerned is the primary reference point, whereas we are more often aware of surrounding forces when we observe ourselves. According to J. G. Miller, the more individualistic the society, the more likely it is to commit the fundamental attribution error—which clearly puts the art world into an extreme category of its own.

The silence surrounding Jason Rhoades's recent passing is just such a case. Despite his autopsy revealing that a large number of prescription and other drugs contributed to his heart failure, information that is now a matter of public record, no one in the established art world dared mentioned it, presumably to avoid attracting bad press. Without mentioning the negative impact of such publicity on future gallery sales, the suspicion exists that this silence was largely a defense mechanism, sanctifying fallen angels via the abjuration of the art world's own less-than-upright behavior. Leaving aside the medieval manner in which the art world chooses to brook no opposition, Jason's death was a completely wasted opportunity to understand and avoid denial.

This interview represents responses, written between February 3 and February 25, 2008, to a set questionnaire supplied by Simon Rees

The Covers

1

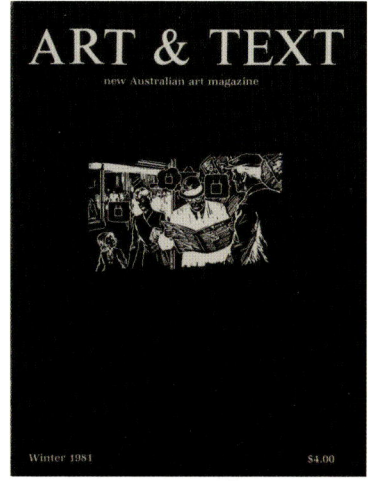

2

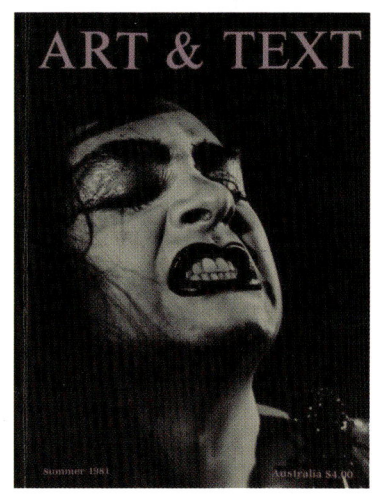

3

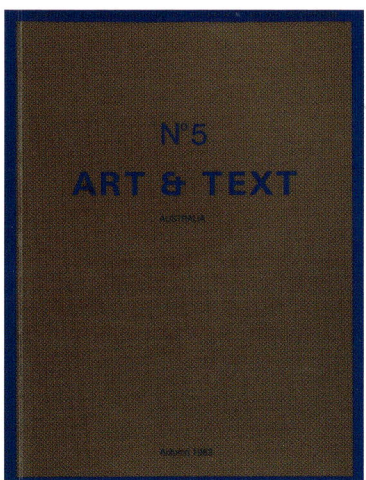

4

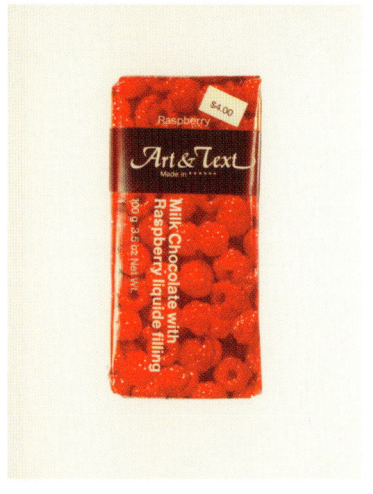

5

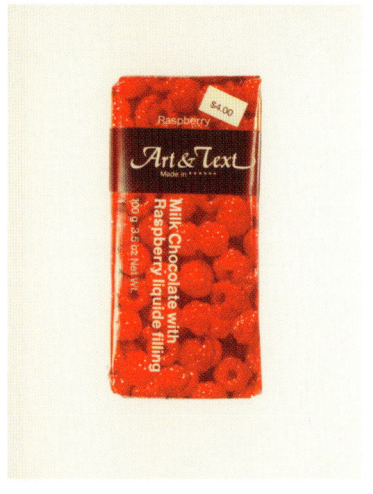

6

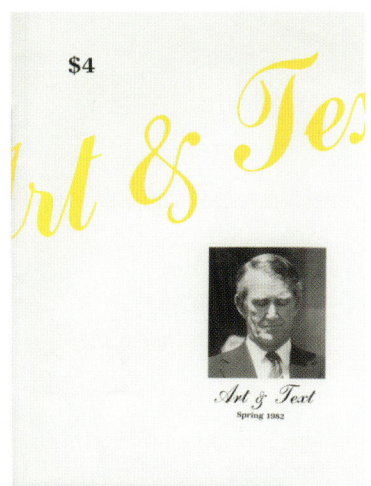

$4

Art & Text
Spring 1982

7

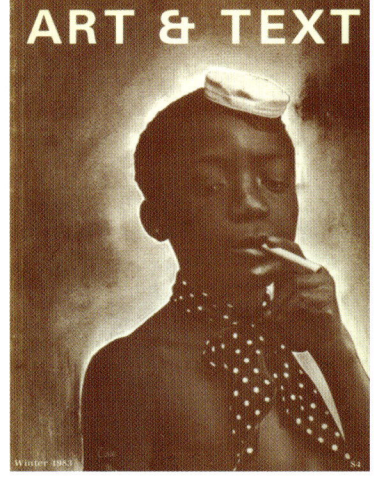

ART & TEXT

WHAT IS
THE USE OF
INTELLECTUALS ?

POOL-SIDE ISSUE
$4

8

ART & TEXT

Autumn 1983
Edited by Paul Taylor

$4

IMAGE SCAVENGERS   9

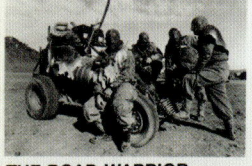

THE ROAD WARRIOR
THE GOOD OIL COMPANY
AND THE BAD OIL COMPANY
G. CELANT: FLASHBACK ON D-7
M. SERRES: LAUGHS: THE
MISAPPROPRIATED JEWELS
P. MARCHANT: ON THE USE OF
CERTAIN WORDS
L. JONES: PREDICTION PIECE # 9

9

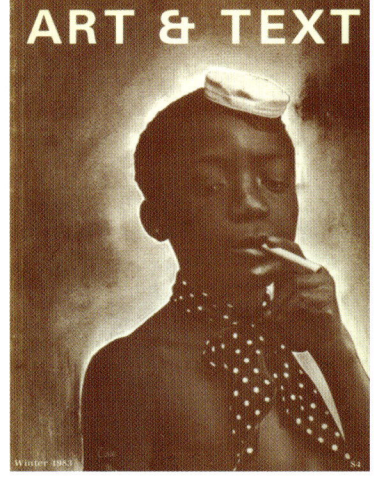

ART & TEXT

Winter 1983 $4

10

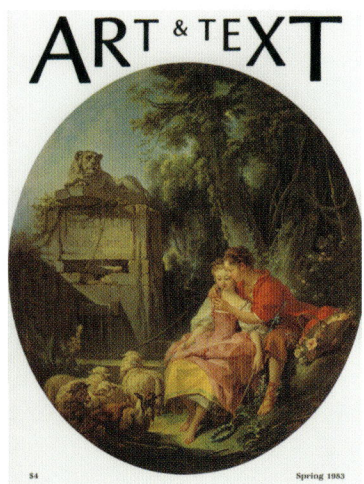

ART & TEXT

$4   Spring 1983

11

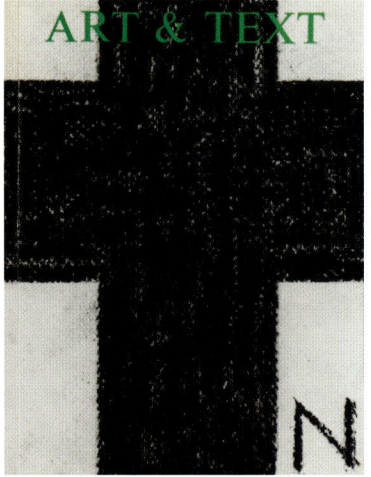

ART & TEXT

12/13

14

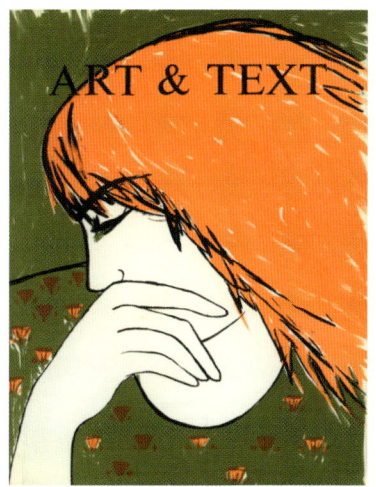

15

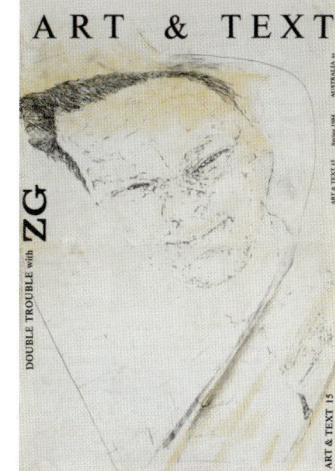

16

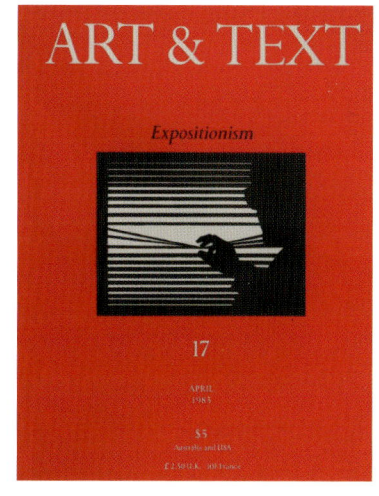

17

18

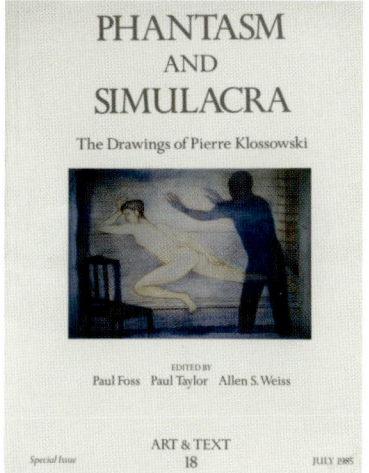

19

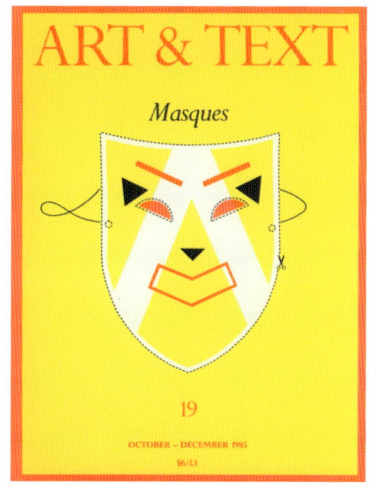

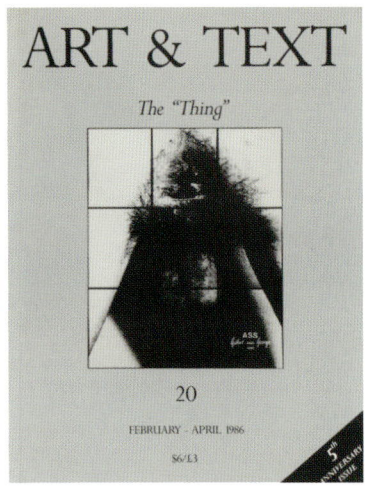

20

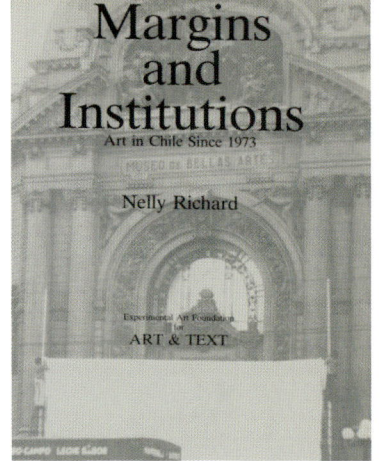

21

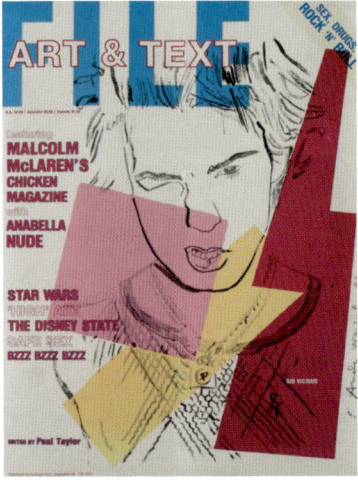

22

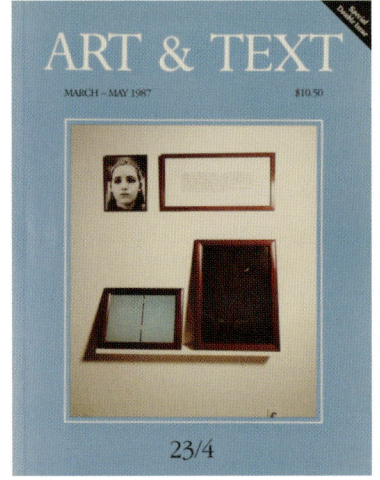

23/24

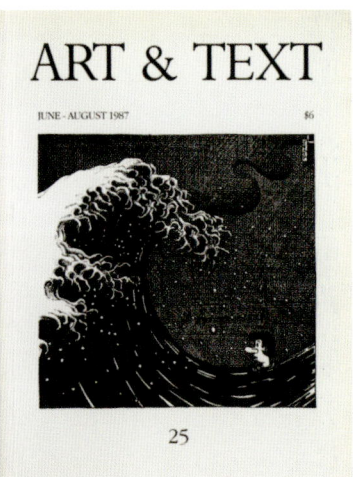

25

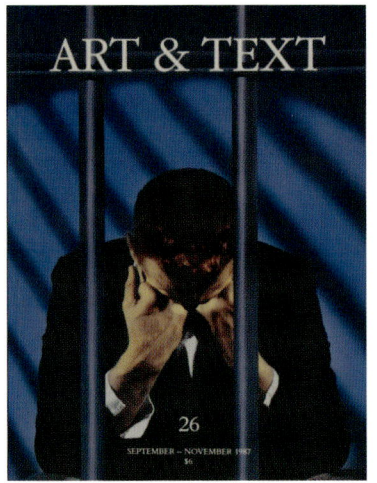

26

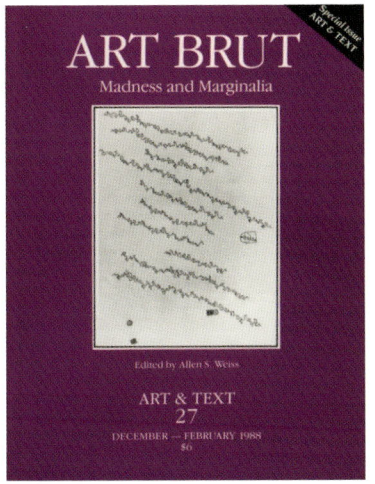

27

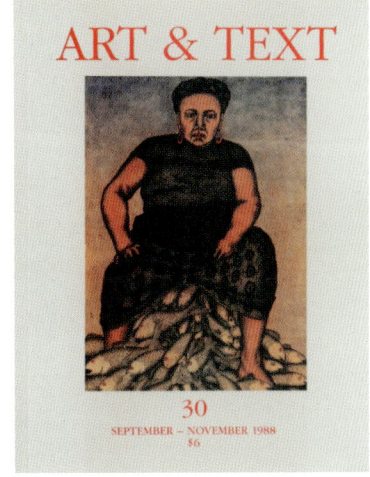

28

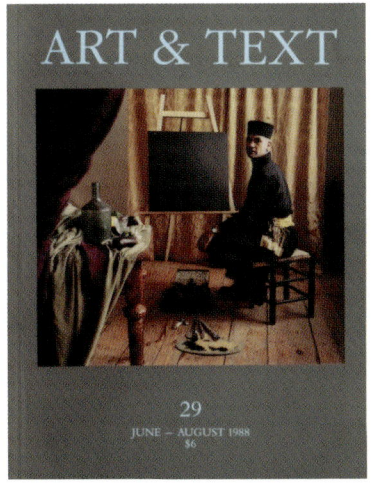

29

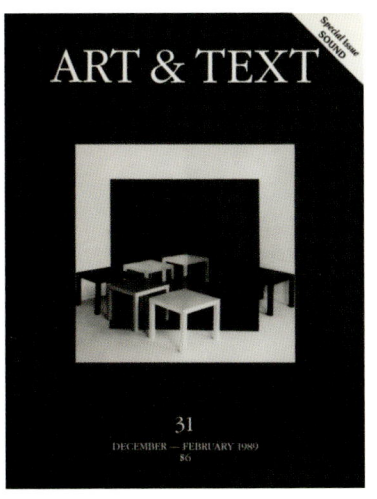

30

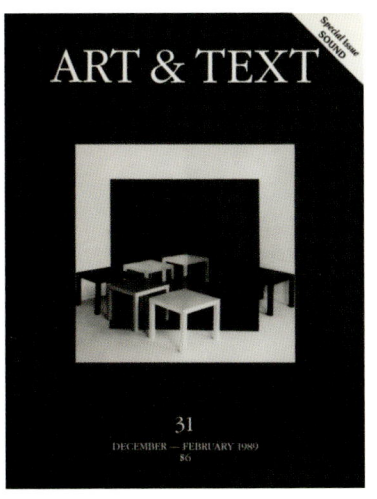

31

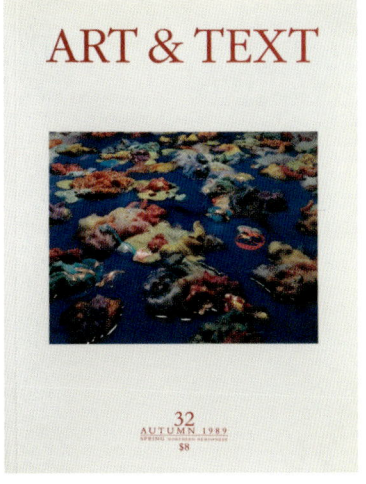

32

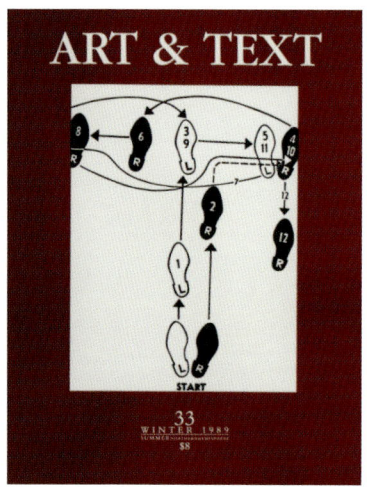

33

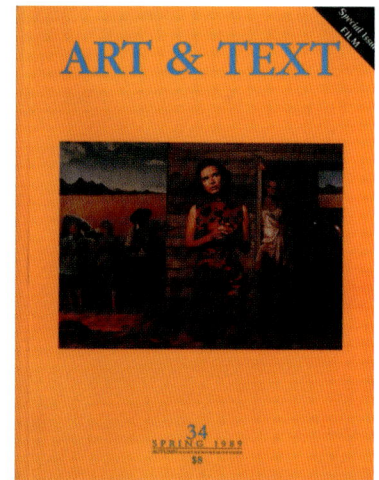

34

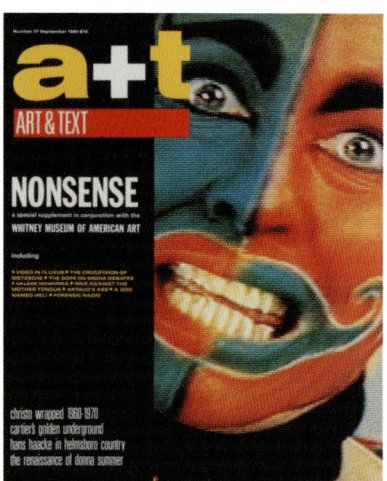

35

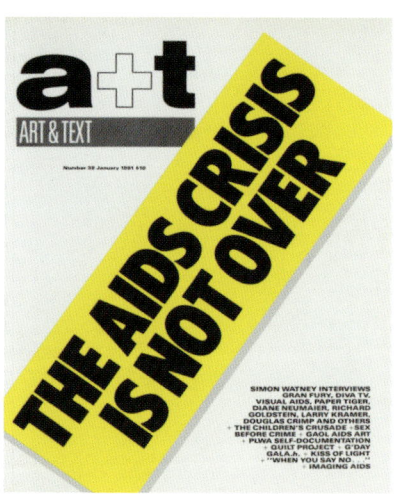

36

37

38

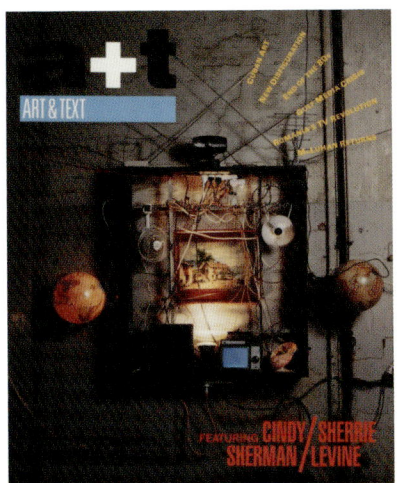

39

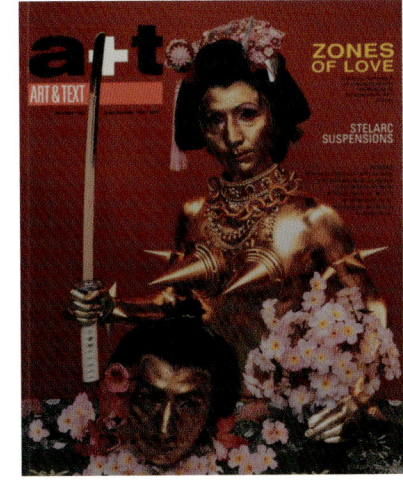

40

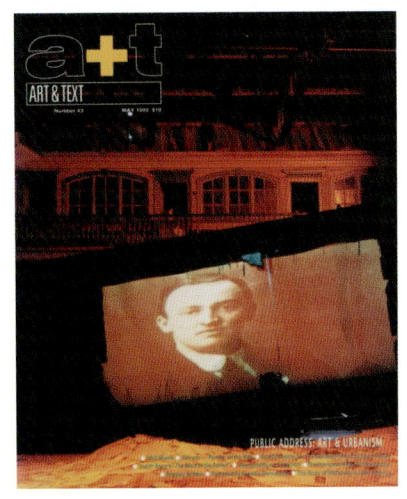

42

41

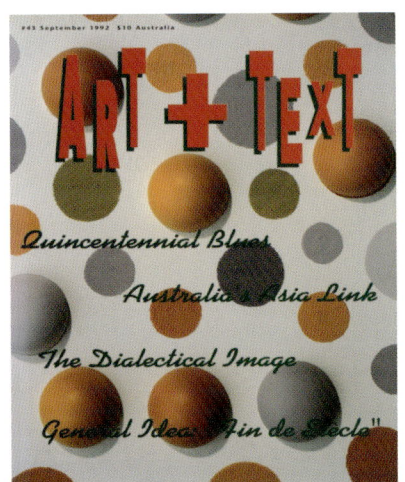

43

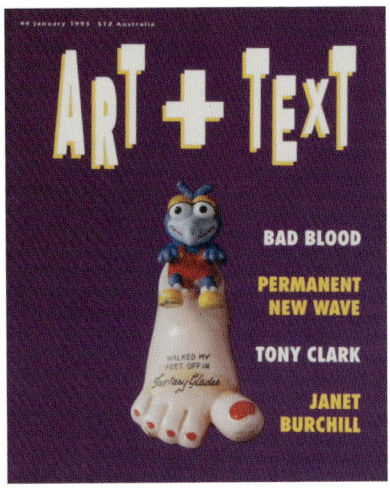

44

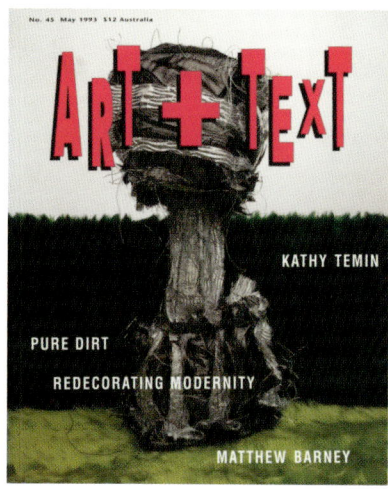

45

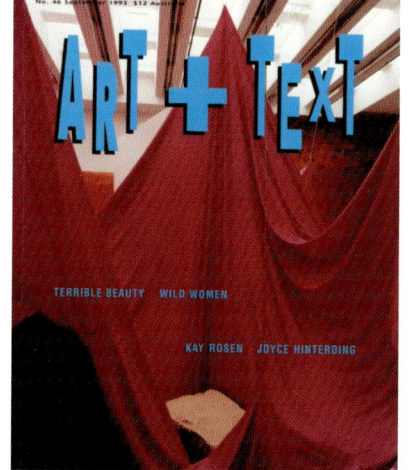

46

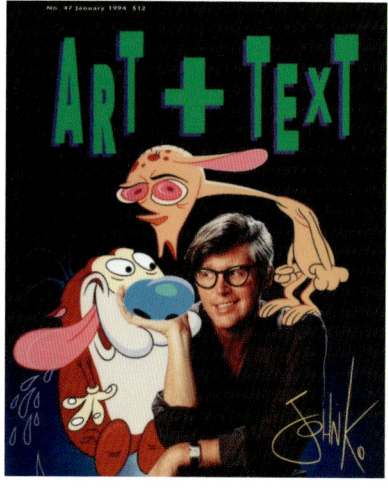

47

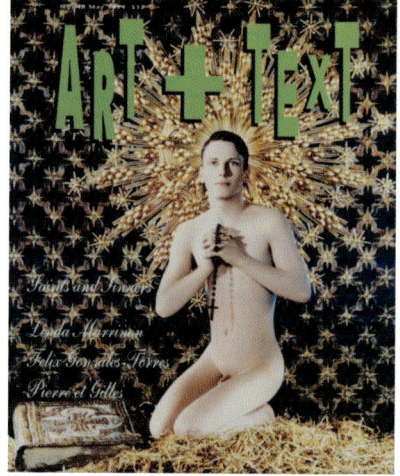

48

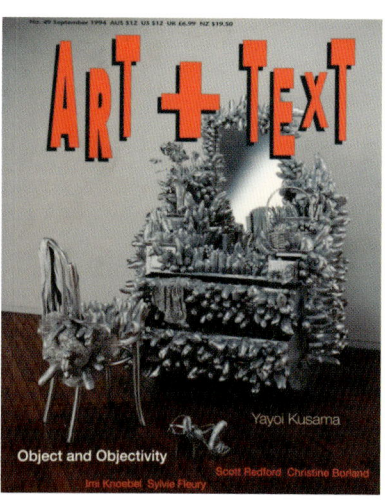

49

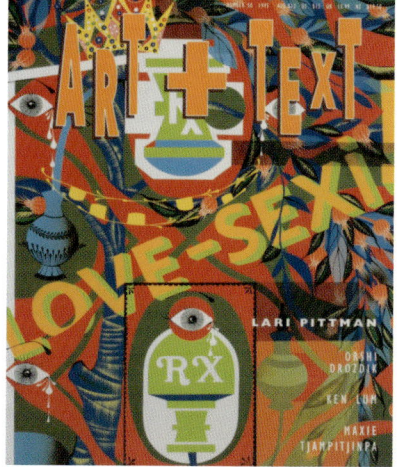

50

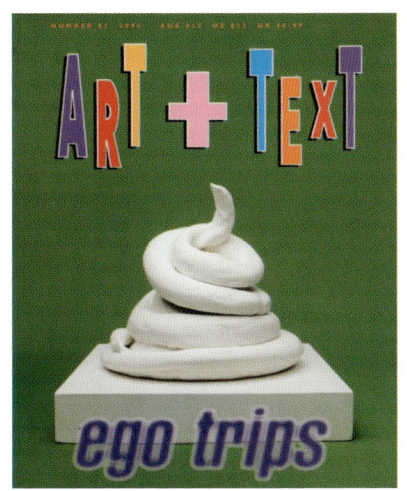

51

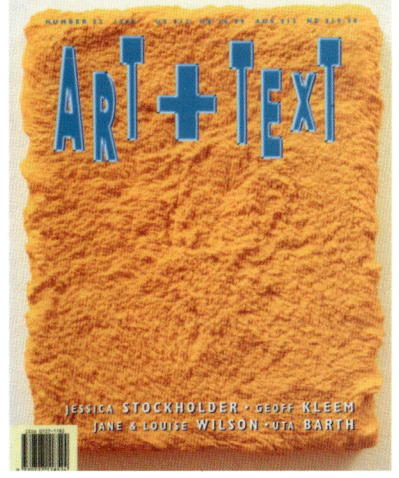

52

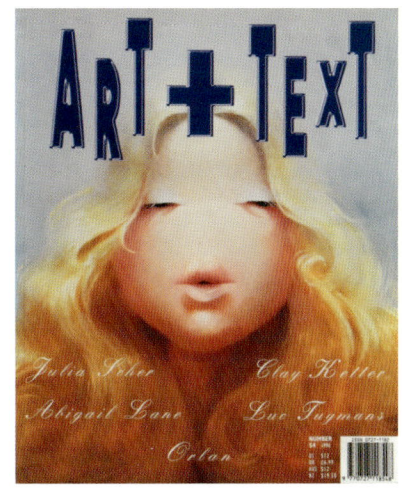

53

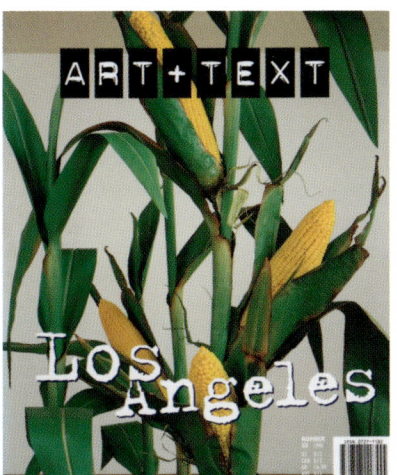

54

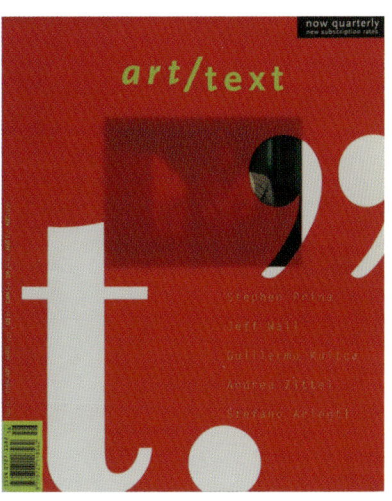

55

56

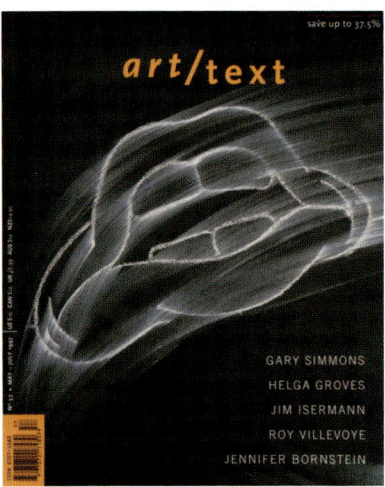

57

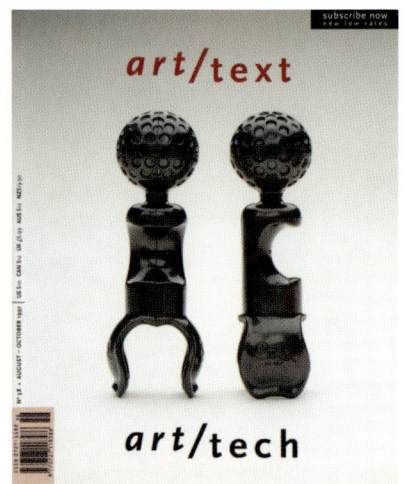

58

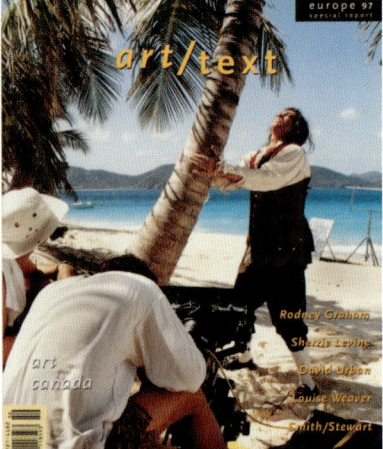

59

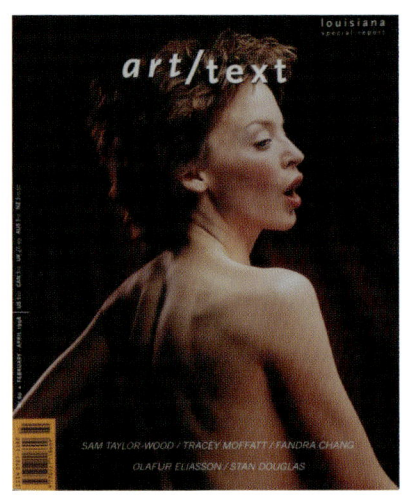

60

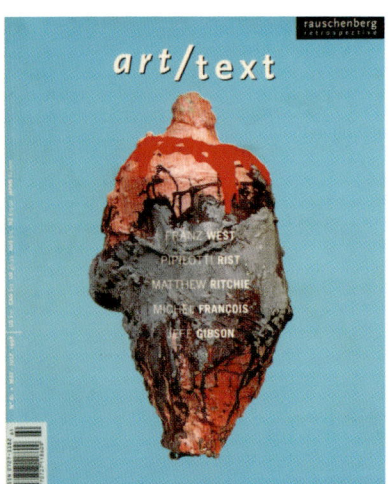

61

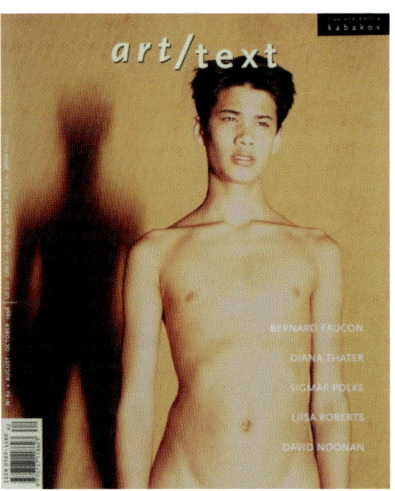

62

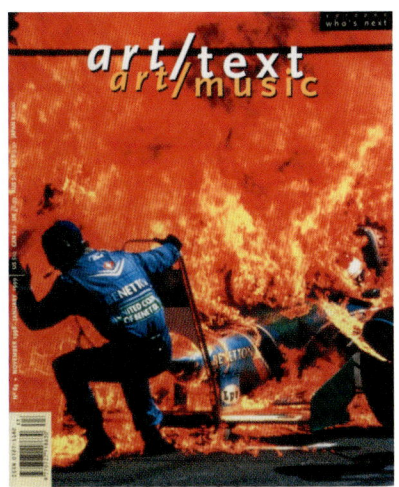

63

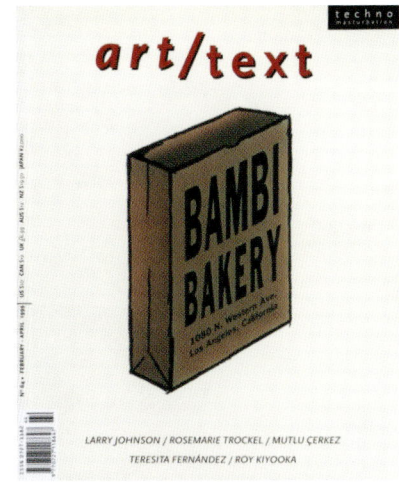

64

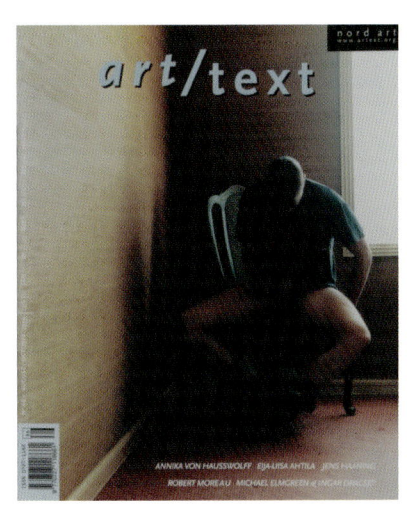

65

66

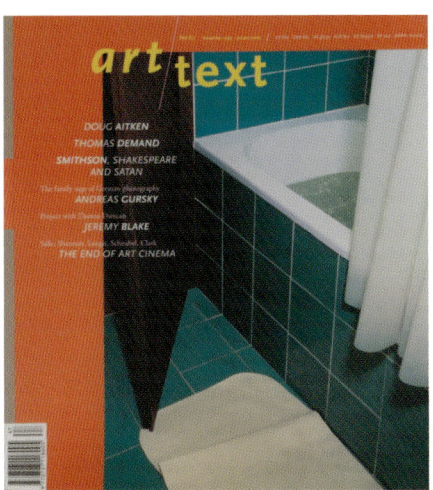

67

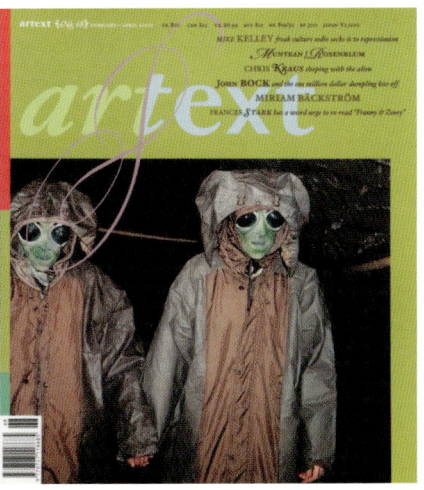

68

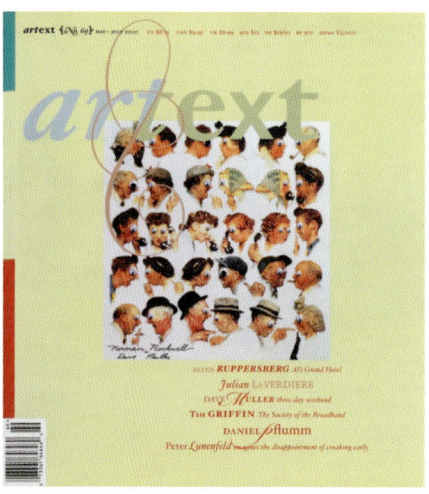

69

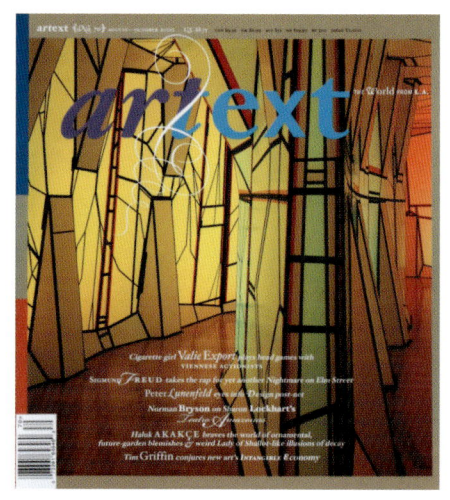

70

71

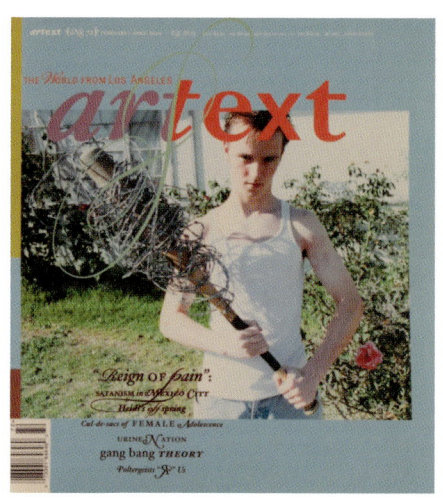

72

73

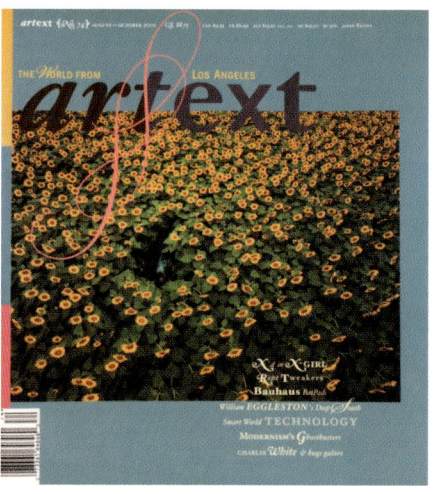

74

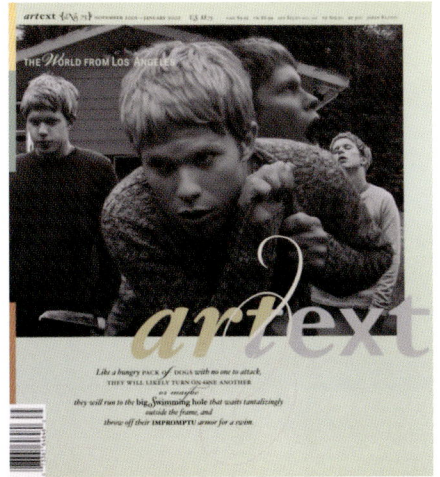

75

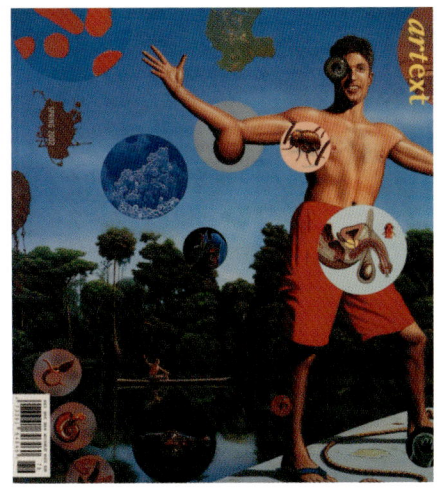

76

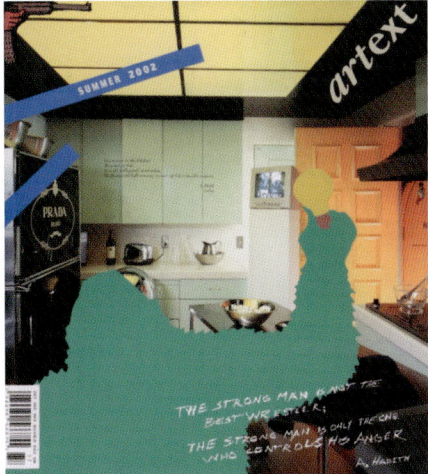

77

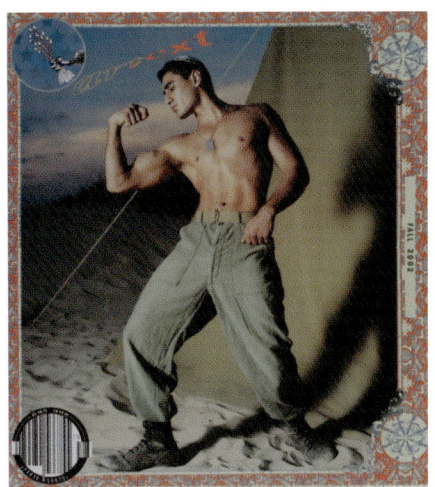

78

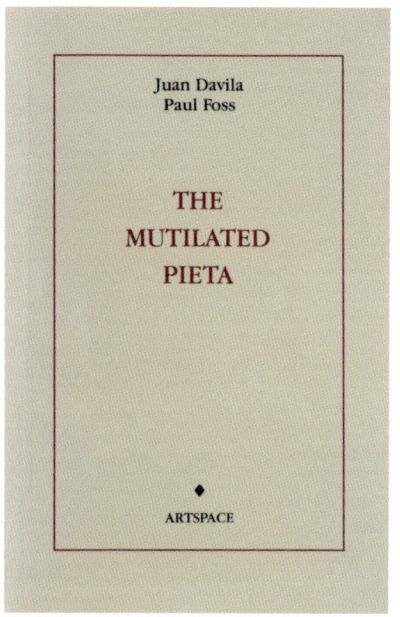

Juan Davila
Paul Foss

THE
MUTILATED
PIETA

◆

ARTSPACE

1985

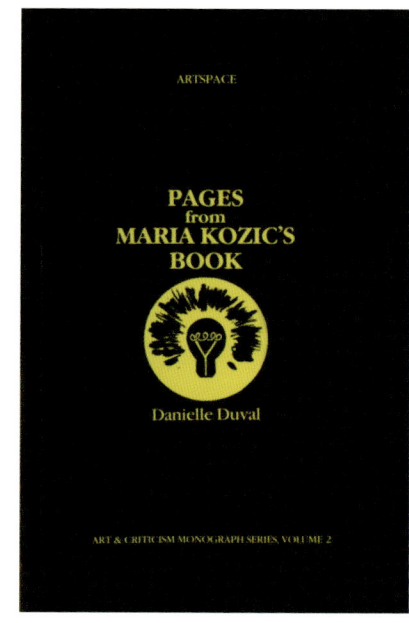

ARTSPACE

PAGES
from
MARIA KOZIC'S
BOOK

Danielle Duval

ART & CRITICISM MONOGRAPH SERIES, VOLUME 2

1987

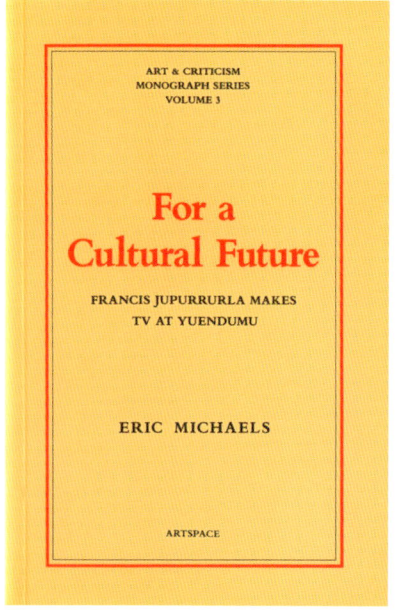

ART & CRITICISM
MONOGRAPH SERIES
VOLUME 3

For a
Cultural Future

FRANCIS JUPURRURLA MAKES
TV AT YUENDUMU

ERIC MICHAELS

ARTSPACE

1987

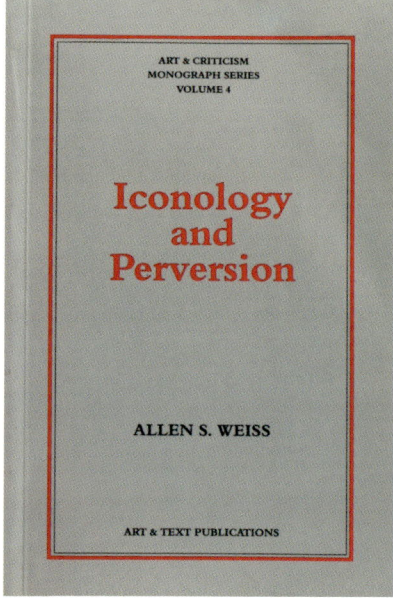

ART & CRITICISM
MONOGRAPH SERIES
VOLUME 4

Iconology
and
Perversion

ALLEN S. WEISS

ART & TEXT PUBLICATIONS

1988

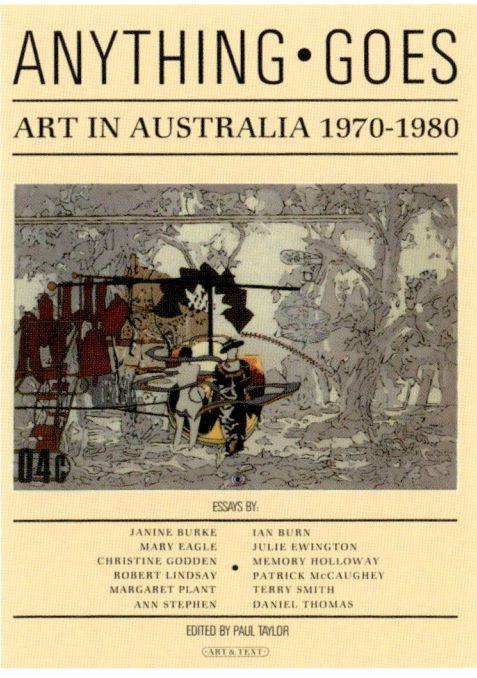

ANYTHING·GOES

ART IN AUSTRALIA 1970-1980

ESSAYS BY:

JANINE BURKE   IAN BURN
MARY EAGLE   JULIE EWINGTON
CHRISTINE GODDEN   MEMORY HOLLOWAY
ROBERT LINDSAY   ·   PATRICK McCAUGHEY
MARGARET PLANT   TERRY SMITH
ANN STEPHEN   DANIEL THOMAS

EDITED BY PAUL TAYLOR

ART & TEXT

1984

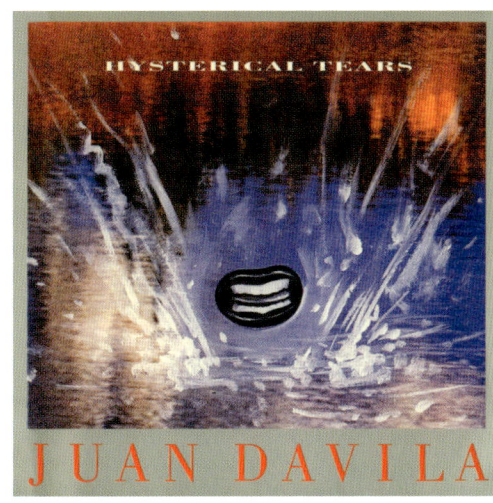

HYSTERICAL TEARS

JUAN DAVILA

1985

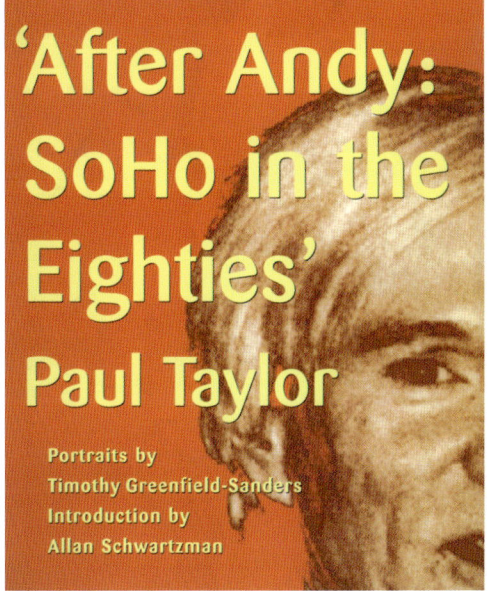

'After Andy:
SoHo in the
Eighties'
Paul Taylor

Portraits by
Timothy Greenfield-Sanders
Introduction by
Allan Schwartzman

1995

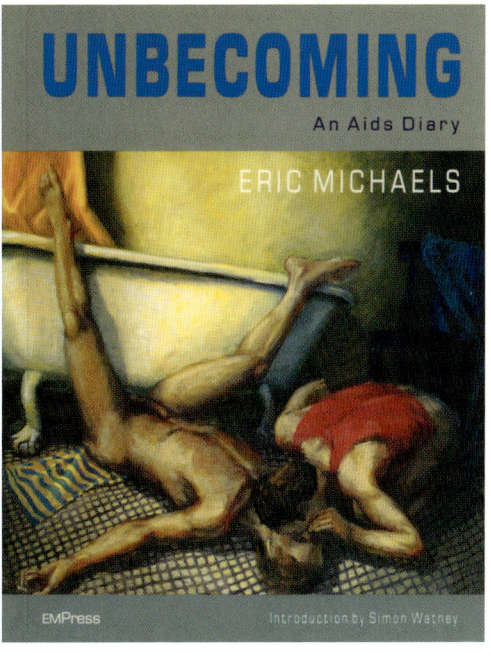

UNBECOMING
An Aids Diary

ERIC MICHAELS

EMPress   Introduction by Simon Watney

1997

ART + TEXT — 51 — MAY 1995

ART + TEXT — 52 — SEPTEMBER 1995

ART + TEXT — 53 — JANUARY 1996

ART + TEXT — 54 — MAY 1996

ART + TEXT — 55 — OCTOBER 1996

N° 56 — ART+TEXT — FEBRUARY – APRIL 1997 — STEPHEN PRINA · JEFF WALL · GUILLERMO KUITCA · ANDREA ZITTEL · STEFANO ARIENTI

N° 57 — art/text — MAY – JULY 1997 — GARY SIMMONS · HELGA GROVES · JIM ISERMANN · ROY VILLEVOYE · JENNIFER BORNSTEIN

N° 58 — art/text — AUGUST – OCTOBER 1997 — MICHAEL JOAQUIN GREY · JENNIFER STEINKAMP · DAMIEN HIRST · CHRIS OFILI · MARGARET MORGAN

N° 59 — art/text — NOVEMBER 1997 – JANUARY 1998 — RODNEY GRAHAM · SHERRIE LEVINE · DAVID URBAN · LOUISE WEAVER · SMITH/STEWART

N° 60 — art/text — FEBRUARY – APRIL 1998 — SAM TAYLOR-WOOD · TRACEY MOFFATT · FANDRA CHANG · OLAFUR ELIASSON · STAN DOUGLAS

N° 61 — art/text — MAY – JULY 1998 — FRANZ WEST · PIPILOTTI RIST · MATTHEW RITCHIE · MICHEL FRANÇOIS · JEFF GIBSON

N° 62 — art/text — AUGUST – OCTOBER 1998 — BERNARD FAUCON · DIANA THATER · SIGMAR POLKE · LIISA ROBERTS · DAVID NOONAN

N° 63 — art/text — NOVEMBER 1998 – JANUARY 1999 — ISAAC JULIEN · SAM DURANT · ROSEMARY LAING · STEPHEN BIRCH · DAVID BUNN

N° 64 — art/text — FEBRUARY – APRIL 1999 — LARRY JOHNSON · ROSEMARIE TROCKEL · MUTLU ÇERKEZ · TERESITA FERNÁNDEZ · ROY KIYOOKA

N° 65 — art/text — MAY – JULY 1999 — SARAH SZE · OLIVER HERRING · EDWARD LIPSKY · KIM SOO-JA · CHRISTOPHER LANGTON

N° 66 — art/text — AUGUST – OCTOBER 1999 — ANNIKA VON HAUSSWOLFF · EIJA-LIISA AHTILA · JENS HAANING · ROBERT MOREAU · MICHAEL ELMGREEN & INGAR DRAGSET

N° 67 — artext — DOUG AITKEN · THOMAS DEMAND · ANDREAS GURSKY · JEREMY BLAKE THE END OF ART CINEMA · SMITHSON, SHAKESPEARE & SATAN

N° 68 — artext — Mike KELLEY · MUNTEAN/ROSENBLUM · John BOCK · Shirley TSE · Joachim KOESTER · Miriam BÄCKSTRÖM · Hany ARMANIOUS

N° 69 — artext — Al RUPPERSBERG · Julian LAVERDIERE · Ashley BICKERTON · Dave MULLER · Daniel PFLUMM · Kathy TEMIN

artext N° 70 — Sharon LOCKHART · Haluk AKAKCE · Oleg BREUNING · Adam ROSS · Velika EXPORT · Daniel MALONE

artext N° 71 — 9011 art in LOS ANGELES · Karen YASINSKY · Philip TAAFFE · Albert OEHLEN · Nic HESS · Ulrike OTTINGER

N° 72 — Girls by GIRLS · Julia BECKER · Evan HOLLOWAY · Angus FAIRHURST · Miguel CALDERON · Mee-Lee CHEANG

The ART & TEXT Library

Organized by Rob McKenzie

David McNeill, "Body," 81–82.
Jacqueline Millner, "Bronia Iwanczak," 82–83.
Shane Breynard, "Archives & the Everyday," 83–84.
Stuart Koop, "Diorama," 84–85.
Robert Schubert, "Birgitta Muhr, Alex Rizkalla," 85–86.
D.J. Huppatz, "Deborah Ostrow, Brett Valance," 86–87.
Robert Leonard, "Gavin Hipkins," 87–88.
Susan Dewar, "Sui Jianguo, Li Gang," 88–89.
Robert Fouser, "1997 Kwangju Biennale," 89–90.
Barbara U. Schmidt, "Steirischer Herbst '97," 91–92.
Stephen Todd, "Marylène Negro," 92–93.
David Barrett, "Sensation," 93–94.
Elisabeth Mahoney, "Shane Cullen," 94–95.
Elizabeth Hayt, "Dinos and Jake Chapman," 95–96.
Saul Anton, "In-Form," 96–97.
Ihor Holubizky, "Barbara Astman," 97.
Marcia Tanner, "Dominique Blain," 98.
Christopher Miles, "Robert Gober," 99.
David Pagel, "Kim Dingle," 100.
Mario Cutajar, "Nancy Davidson," 100–101.

Issue 61, May–July 1998, Sydney/Los Angeles (director Paul Foss, editor Susan Kandel)
BOOKS
Susan Kandel, "Turnstile Gothic," 26–27.
COMMENTS
Liz Kotz, "Amy Adler: Surrogates," 28–31.
Terry R. Myers, "Pipilotti Rist: Grist for the Mill," 32–35.
Stuart Koop, "Kate Beynon: New Foreign Language," 36–39.
Jan Tumlir, "Pae White: The Nouveau Objet," 40–43.
APROPOS
Jonathan Katz, "Rauschenberg's Honeymoon," 44–47.
PROJECT
Marilu Knode, "Tony Tasset," 48–53.
FEATURES
Jeffrey Kastner, "The Weather of Chance: Matthew Ritchie and the Butterfly Effect," 54–59.
Giorgio Verzotti, "Franz West: Fitting Parts," 60–65.
Thomas W. Sokolowski, "Jeff Gibson: Say My Name," 66–71.
Frank-Alexander Hettig, "Michel François: Nothing in My Pockets," tr. Jeremy Gaines, 72–77.
REPORT
David Pagel, "Out of Actions," 78–79.
REVIEWS
Christopher Miles, "Tim Hawkinson," 80.
Peter Lunenfeld, "Bill Viola," 80–81.
Giovanni Intra, "Frances Stark," 82–83.
Ihor Holubizky, "Up North," 83–84.
Scott Watson, "Kate Craig," 84–85.
Saul Anton, "Oliver Herring," 85–86.
Elizabeth Hayt, "Paul Shambroom," 86.
Megan Ratner, "Marina Abramović," 87.
Jen Budney, "Johannesburg Biennale 1997," 88–89.
David Barrett, "Gregor Schneider," 89–90.
Mats Stjernstedt, "Stig Sjölund," tr. Jan Teeland, 90–91.
Charles Green, "9th Triennale-India," 91–92.
Robert Fouser, "Yukinori Yanagi," 92–93.
Christina Barton, "Alt.nature," 93–94.
Rex Butler, "Francesco Conz and the Intermedia Avant-garde," 94–95.
Julie Ewington, "Yves Klein," 96–97.
Alex Gawronski, "Elvis Richardson, Mark Hislop," 97–98.
Blair French, "Maria Cruz," 98–99.
Jacqueline Millner, "Suburban Fetish," 99–100.
Stephen O'Connell, "General Review of Gain and Loss," 100–101.
Stuart Koop, "Andrew Hurle," 101.

Issue 62, August–October 1998, Sydney/Los Angeles (director Paul Foss, editor Susan Kandel)
BOOKS
Lee Smith, "Beyond Love and Dick," 26–27.
COMMENTS
Saul Anton, "Liisa Roberts: Time Machines," 28–31.
Juliana Engberg, "Ricky Swallow: No Radio," 32–35.
Ihor Holubizky, "Micah Lexier: Life Expectancy," 36–38.
Sue Spaid, "Caren Furbeyre: Shaken Not Stirred," 39–41.
APROPOS
Jeremy Gilbert-Rolfe, "Notes on Being Framed by a Surface," 42–45.
PROJECT
Bruce Hainley, "Richard Hawkins: Starfucker," 46–51.
FEATURES
Stephen Todd, "Bernard Faucon: Frigid Image," 52–57.
David Moos, "Clairvoyant Memories: The Time of Sigmar Polke," 58–65.
Peter Lunenfeld, "Diana Thater: Constraint Decree," 66–72.
Stephen O'Connell, "David Noonan: Metaphysical Bodysuits," 73–77.
REPORT
Barry Schwabsky, "Ilya & Emilia Kabakov," 78–79.
REVIEWS
Michael Corris, "Graham Ellard / Stephen Johnstone," 80–81.
Sue Spaid, "Fellessentralen," 81–82.
Terry R. Myers, "Thomas Ruff," 82–83.
Jane Harris, "Marie José Burki," 83–84.
Regine Basha, "Omar Lopez-Chahoud," 84–85.
Barry Schwabsky, "Inka Essenhigh," 85–86.
Michelle Grabner, "Dave Deany," 86–87.
Ryan Whyte, "Points of View," 87–88.
Christopher Miles, "Sharon Lockhart," 88–89.
Mario Cutajar, "Jeremy Kidd," 89–90.
Jan Tumlir, "Uta Barth," 90–92.
Keith Miller, "Ridiculum Vitae," 92.
Felipe Chaimovich, "Iran Espírito Santo," 93.
Rex Butler, "Emily Kngwarreye," 94–95.
Blair French, "1998 Adelaide Biennial of Australian Art," 95–97.
Charles Green, "Construction in Process VI," 97–98.
Felicity Colman, "Kathy Temin," 98–99.
D.J. Huppatz, "Andrea Blundell and Nadine Christensen," 99.
Benjamin Genocchio, "Arabmade," 100.
Jacqueline Millner, "William Seeto," 101.
Robert Fouser, "Kho Nak–beom," 102.

Issue 63 (subtitled: "Art/Music"), November 1998–January 1999, Sydney/Los Angeles (director Paul Foss, editor Susan Kandel)
COLUMNS
Chris Kraus, "Let's Call the Whole Thing Off," 24–26.
Liam Gillick, "So There Are at Least Two Types of Lobby," 26–28.
Peter Lunenfeld, "Permanent Presence," 28–30.
COMMENTS
Blair French, "Stephen Birch: Outcasts," 31–33.
Jan Tumlir, "David Bunn: Bureaucratic Poetry," 34–37.
Evelyn McDonnell, "Wham, Glam, Thank You Ma'am," 38–41.
Jozef van Wissem and Mariah Corrigan, "Euro Vision," 42–44.
APROPOS
Greg Siegel, " 'Who's Next': Preserving Originality in Systems of Seriality," 45–47.
PROJECT
Christopher Miles, "Sam Durant: Going with the Flow," 48–53.
FEATURES
Michael Corris, "Heavenly Bodies in Motion: Isaac Julien's Queer Trilogy," 54–59.
Laurence A. Rickels, "Phantoms of Opera," 60–66.
Annemarie Jonson, "Rosemary Laing: Stall Fall," 67–73.

Simon Rees, "Dale Frank," 80.
Rachel Kushner, "Aidas Bareikas," 81.
Mark von Schlegell, "Yuki Kimura," 82.
Margaret Morgan, "Narelle Jubelin/Marcos Corrales Lantero," 83.
Gavin Hipkins, "Ken Lum," 83–84.
David Hunt, "Ester Partegas," 84–85.
Michael Turner, "These Days," 85.
Stuart Koop, "Slave Pianos," 86.
Trevor Mahovsky, "David Hoffos," 87.
Malik Gaines, "Nils Norman," 88.
Laurence A. Rickels, "Stephanie Taylor," 88–89.
Jane Harris, "Jacqueline Bootier," 89–90.
Terry R. Myers, "Tyler Vlahovich," 90–91.

Issue 76, Spring 2002, Los Angeles (publisher Paul Foss)
TALK
Matthew DeBord, "Heavy-Tech Lives On," 18.
Peter Lunenfeld, "Anthropomorphometric," 20.
Terry R. Myers, "Unpacking L.A.'s Library," 22–23.
Randy Gladman, "Alexis Rockman," 24–25.
Kelly Wood, "The Death Agony of Jeff Wall," 26–27.
David Hunt, "Luis Gispert: Benediction, or Beatdown?", 28.
PROJECT
Giovanni Intra, "De Rijke/De Rooij," 30–35.
FEATURES
Jan Tumlir, "Dave Hullfish Bailey: Visitation Rites," 36–45.
John Kelsey, "Carey Young: Business As Usual," 46–49.
Giovanni Intra, "Lisa Lapinski: Sculpturicide," 50–55.
David Hunt, "Jim Lambie: Unlofty Means," 56–63.
Clare Manchester, "Mike Nelson: Uroboros of Illusion," 64–69.
Alex Coles, "Julian Opie's Feel-Good Landscapes," 70–77.
REVIEWS
Terry R. Myers, "The Americans: New Art," 80–81.
Malik Gaines, "Delia Brown," 80–81.
Stuart Koop, "Louisa Bufardeci," 82–83.
Dan Fox, "Richard Wentworth, Eugène Atget," 82–83.
David Spalding, "John Bankston," 82–83.
Malik Gaines, "Michael Minelli," 84–85.
Rachel Kushner, "Jason Middlebrook," 84–85.
James Scarborough, "Sarah Perry," 84–85.
Vincent Pécoil, "Lothar Hempel," tr. Paul Foss, 86–87.
Jeffrey Kastner, "Robert Fischer," 86–87.
David Bussel, "David Musgrave," 86–87.
Kristina Newhouse, "Rachel Lachowicz," 88–89.
Reid Shier, "Steven Shearer," 88–89.
John Slyce, "Cathy Wilkes," 88–89.
Paul Foss, "Ehren Tool," 90–91.
Jane Harris, "Jason Salavon," 90–91.
Tim Griffin, "Rico Gatson," 90–91.

Issue 77, Summer 2002, Los Angeles (editor Paul Foss)
TALK
Giovanni Intra, "Warhol Unbalanced," 28–29.
Matthew DeBord, "Wasted Threads," 30.
Robert Linsley, "Negation: Abstraction in the Era of Religious War," 32–33.
Jan Tumlir, "The Locust Days of Burnett Miller," 34–35.
Malik Gaines, "Julie Mehretu: Aftershocks," 36–37.
PROJECT
David Hunt, "Bigert & Bergström: No Soliciting," 38–43.
FEATURES
Jane Harris, "Nikki S. Lee: When in Rome," 44–47.
Vincent Pécoil, "Öyvind Fahlström: Art's Double Agent," tr. Paul Foss, 48–57.
Laurence A. Rickels, "John Boskovich: North by North," 58–65.
John Slyce, "Paul Noble: Miles From Nowhere," 66–71.
Rachel Kushner, "Scott Reeder: Circling the Square," 72–77.

REVIEWS
Laurence A. Rickels, "Marlene McCarty," 80–81.
Randy Gladman, "Bryan Crockett," 82–83.
JJ Charlesworth, "Play it as it Lays," 82–83.
Susan Corrigan, "Gillian Carnegie," 82–83.
Christina Valentine, "Marion Lane," 84–85.
Emily Pethick, "Josephine Pryde, Barbara Hepworth," 84–85.
David Hunt, "Jeff Elrod," 84–85.
David Hunt, "Daniel Heimbinder," 86–87.
Franklin Sirmans, "Avish Khebrehzadeh," 86–87.
Martha Schwendener, "Carla Klein," 86–87.
James Scarborough, "Alicia Beach," 88–89.
Michelle Grabner, "Gaylen Gerber with Stephen Prina," 88–89.
John Slyce, "Keith Tyson," 88–89.
Giovanni Intra, "Liz Larner," 90–91.
Kristina Newhouse, "Won Ju Lim," 90–91.
Josh Blackwell, "Steven Criqui," 90–91.

Issue 78, Fall 2002, Los Angeles (editor Paul Foss)
TALK
Domenick Ammirati, "Border Bordello," 22–23.
Jane Harris, "Fighting for Love," 24–25.
Giovanni Intra, "Paid in Full," 26–27.
Laurence A. Rickels, "Tom Allen: Becoming Ruin," 28–29.
PROJECT
Sinisa Mitrovic, "Phil Collins: Merry Christmas Mr. Collins," 30–35.
FEATURES
JJ Charlesworth, "Mute Matter and Stuttering Machines: Sign and Substance in Recent Sculpture," 36–43.
Christopher Miles, "Mark Grotjahn: Working Variables, Switching Games," 44–51.
Kirsty Bell, "Björn Darlem: Bad Science," 52–57.
David Hunt, "Torben Giehler: Shockwave Xanadu," 58–63.
Jan Tumlir, "Morbid Curiosity: The Art School Curriculum and Modernism Unbound," 64–76.
REVIEWS
Domenick Ammirati, "Whitney Biennial 2002," 78–79.
Terry R. Myers, "Documenta 11," 80–81.
Paul Foss, "Adi Nes," 80–81.
Michael Rush, "Matthew Barney," 82–83.
Alex Coles, "David Batchelor," 82–83.
David Hunt, "Jonathan Calm," 82–83.
Malik Gaines, "J.P. Munro," 84–85.
Eve Wood, "Chris Johanson," 84–85.
David Hunt, "Daniela Rossell," 84–85.
Dustin Ericksen, "A Short History of Performance: Part One," 86–87.
Emily Pethick, "Christina Mackie," 86–87.
Susan Corrigan, "Georgina Starr," 86–87.
Jeffrey Kastner, "Marina Kappos," 88–89.
Ken Gonzales-Day, "Daniel J. Martinez," 88–89.
Randy D. Gladman, "Daniel Roth," 88–89.
Kristina Newhouse, "Frances Stark," 90–91.
Catherine Wood, "Inframince," 90–91.
Simon Rees, "Bittersweet," 90–91.

Bibliographies

Paul Taylor

Popism, exhibition catalogue (Melbourne: National Gallery of Victoria, 1982).

Tall Poppies, exhibition catalogue (Melbourne: University Gallery, University of Melbourne, 1983).

"Frances Lindsay and Paul Groot," in *Dale Frank*, exhibition catalogue (Melbourne: University Gallery, University of Melbourne, 1984).

Anything Goes: Art in Australia 1970–1980, ed. Paul Taylor (Melbourne: Art & Text, 1984).

Hysterical Tears: Juan Davila, ed. Paul Taylor (Melbourne: Greenhouse Publications, 1985).

Impresario: Malcolm McLaren and the British New Wave, exhibition catalogue (New York/Cambridge, Mass.: New Museum of Contemporary Art/MIT Press, 1988).

Post-Pop Art, ed. Paul Taylor (Cambridge, Mass: MIT Press, 1989).

After Andy: SoHo in the Eighties, organized by Paul Foss (Melbourne: Schwartz City, 1995).

Paul Foss

Language, Sexuality & Subversion, eds. Paul Foss and Meaghan Morris (Sydney: Feral, 1978). Contributor and translator.

Michel Foucault: Power, Truth, Strategy, eds. Meaghan Morris and Paul Patton (Sydney: Feral, 1979). Contributor and translator.

Fassbinder in Review: An Appreciation of the Cinema of Rainer Werner Fassbinder, ed. Paul Foss (Sydney and Melbourne: Australian Film Institute, 1983).

Jean Baudrillard, *Simulations*, tr. Paul Foss, Paul Patton, and Philip Beitchman (New York: Semiotext(e), 1983).

Jean Baudrillard, *In the Shadow of the Silent Majorities*, tr. Paul Foss, Paul Patton, and John Johnston (New York: Semiotext(e), 1983).

Hysterical Tears: Juan Davila, ed. Paul Taylor (Melbourne: Greenhouse, 1985). Contributor and translator.

Phantasm and Simulacra: The Drawings of Pierre Klossowski, eds. Paul Foss and Allen S. Weiss, *Art & Text* 18 (July 1985).

Juan Davila and Paul Foss, *The Mutilated Pieta* (Sydney: Artspace, 1985).

Nelly Richard, *Margins and Institutions: Art in Chile since 1973*, tr. Paul Foss and Juan Davila, *Art & Text* 21 (May–July 1986).

Danielle Duval (Juan Davila and Paul Foss), *Pages from Maria Kozic's Book* (Melbourne: Art & Criticism Monograph Series, Vol. 2, 1987).

Island in the Stream: Myths of Place in Australian Culture, ed. Paul Foss (Sydney: Pluto Press, 1988).

Jean Baudrillard, *Revenge of the Crystal: Selected Writings on the Modern Object and its Destiny, 1968–1983*, selected and translated by Paul Foss and Julian Pefanis (London/Sydney: Pluto Press/Power Institute of Fine Arts, University of Sydney, 1990).

Eric Michaels, *Bad Aboriginal Art: Tradition, Media, and Technological Horizons*, ed. Paul Foss (Minneapolis: Minnesota University Press, 1994).

Paul Taylor, *After Andy: SoHo in the Eighties*, organized by Paul Foss (Melbourne: Schwartz City, 1995).

Eric Michaels, *Unbecoming*, ed. Paul Foss (Durham: Duke University Press, 1997).

Contributors

PAUL FOSS is the publishing editor of the art magazines *Art & Text* and *artUS*. A renowned translator, anthologist, and author, his publications include *Island in the Stream: Myths of Place in Australian Culture*.

ROSS CHAMBERS, now retired, was Marvin Felheim Distinguished University Professor of French and Comparative Literature at the University of Michigan. His many books include *Loiterature*.

ROB MCKENZIE is a writer and artist and was born in Melbourne, Australia. He makes art collaboratively with Kain Picken and their work is represented by Uplands Gallery, Melbourne. He has worked on independent publications in collaboration with artists and designers including Ester Partegas and Bless. He currently lives in New York.

REX BUTLER is an Associate Professor in the School of English, Media Studies, and Art History at the University of Queensland, Brisbane. He has written studies of Jean Baudrilliard and Slavoj Žižek and written and edited books on Australian art. His forthcoming book is the edited collection *Jeremy Gilbert Rolfe: Art after Deconstruction*.

SIMON REES is a curator at the Contemporary Art Centre in Vilnius, Lithuania, where he is commissioning curator of the international lecture series CAC Cafe Talks and co-editor of the bilingual magazine *Interviu: The Quarterly Conversation about Art*. He is currently working on two major projects for the *Vilnius: European Capital of Culture 2009* program. Before moving to Europe, he was curator at the Govett-Brewster Art Gallery, New Plymouth, and Artspace, Sydney, before which he was managing editor of *Art & Text* in Sydney.

Paul Foss et al
The &-Files: Art & Text 1981-2002
ISBN 978-0-9799752-1-9
Library of Congress Control Number 2009920899

Supported by the Australia Council.

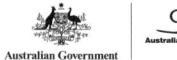

Distributed in the U.S. by University of Nebraska Press, 1111 Lincoln Mall, Lincoln, Nebraska 68588-0630. www.nebraskapress.unl.edu, Tel: +1 800 755 1105, Fax: +1 800 526 2617.

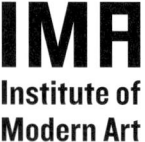

**Institute of
Modern Art**

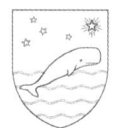

WHALE & STAR

Institute of Modern Art
PO Box 2176
Fortitude Valley BC QLD 4006
Brisbane
Australia
Tel: +61 7 3252 5750
Fax: +61 7 3252 5072
ima@ima.org.au
www.ima.org.au

Whale & Star
648 NE 8th Street
Delray Beach
Florida
33483
United States
info@whaleandstar.com
www.whaleandstar.com

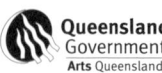
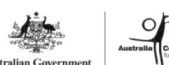

IMA receives financial assistance from the Queensland Government through Arts Queensland (Major Sponsor), from the Visual Arts and Craft Board of the Australia Council (the Federal Government's arts funding and advisory body) and through the Visual Arts And Craft Strategy (an initiative of the Australian, State and Territory Governments). IMA is a member of CAOS, Contemporary Arts Organisations of Australia.